GLOBALVIEWPOINTS

The Global Financial Crisis

Other Books of Related Interest:

At Issue Series

The American Housing Crisis

Introducing Issues with Opposing Viewpoints Series

Globalization

Opposing Viewpoints Series

Consumerism

Debt

The Global Financial Crisis

Noah Berlatsky, Book Editor

GREENHAVEN PRESS

A part of Gale, Cengage Learning

Detroit • New York • San Francisco • New Haven, Conn • Waterville, Maine • London

Christine Nasso, *Publisher*
Elizabeth Des Chenes, *Managing Editor*

© 2010 Greenhaven Press, a part of Gale, Cengage Learning

LIBRARY OF CONGRESS CATALOGING-IN-PUBLICATION DATA

The global financial crisis / Noah Berlatsky, book editor.
    p. cm. -- (Global viewpoints)
    Includes bibliographical references and index.
    ISBN 978-0-7377-4725-6 (hbk.) -- ISBN 978-0-7377-4726-3 (pbk.)
    1. Global financial crisis, 2008-2009--Juvenile literature. 2. Financial crises--Juvenile literature. I. Berlatsky, Noah.
    HB3722.G595 2010
    330.9--dc22

                            2009040550

Printed in the United States of America
1 2 3 4 5 6 7 14 13 12 11 10

Contents

Chapter 2: Effects of the Global Financial Crisis on Wealthier Nations

Chapter 3: Effects of the Global
Financial Crisis on Developing Nations

Chapter 4: Solutions to the Global Financial Crisis

Foreword

*"The problems of all of humanity can
 only be solved by all of humanity."*
—*Swiss author Friedrich Dürrenmatt*

Global interdependence has become an undeniable reality.
Mass media and technology have increased worldwide
access to information and created a society of global citizens.
Understanding and navigating this global community is a
challenge, requiring a high degree of information literacy and
a new level of learning sophistication.

Building on the success of its flagship series, *Opposing
Viewpoints,* Greenhaven Press has created the *Global Viewpoints* series to examine a broad range of current, often controversial topics of worldwide importance from a variety of
international perspectives. Providing students and other readers with the information they need to explore global connec-
tions and think critically about worldwide implications, each
Global Viewpoints volume offers a panoramic view of a topic
of widespread significance.

Drugs, famine, immigration—a broad, international treatment is essential to do justice to social, environmental, health,
and political issues such as these. Junior high, high school,
and early college students, as well as general readers, can all
use *Global Viewpoints* anthologies to discern the complexities
relating to each issue. Readers will be able to examine unique
national perspectives while, at the same time, appreciating the
interconnectedness that global priorities bring to all nations
and cultures.

Material in each volume is selected from a diverse range of
sources, including journals, magazines, newspapers, nonfiction
books, speeches, government documents, pamphlets, organization newsletters, and position papers. *Global Viewpoints* is

truly global, with material drawn primarily from international sources available in English and secondarily from U.S. sources with extensive international coverage.

Features of each volume in the *Global Viewpoints* series include:

- An **annotated table of contents** that provides a brief summary of each essay in the volume, including the name of the country or area covered in the essay.

- An **introduction** specific to the volume topic.

- A **world map** to help readers locate the countries or areas covered in the essays.

- For each viewpoint, an **introduction** that contains notes about the author and source of the viewpoint explains why material from the specific country is being presented, summarizes the main points of the viewpoint, and offers three **guided reading questions** to aid in understanding and comprehension.

- **For further discussion** questions that promote critical thinking by asking the reader to compare and contrast aspects of the viewpoints or draw conclusions about perspectives and arguments.

- A worldwide list of **organizations to contact** for readers seeking additional information.

- A **periodical bibliography** for each chapter and a **bibliography of books** on the volume topic to aid in further research.

- A comprehensive **subject index** to offer access to people, places, events, and subjects cited in the text, with the countries covered in the viewpoints highlighted.

Global Viewpoints is designed for a broad spectrum of readers who want to learn more about current events, history, political science, government, international relations, economics, environmental science, world cultures, and sociology—students doing research for class assignments or debates, teachers and faculty seeking to supplement course materials, and others wanting to understand current issues better. By presenting how people in various countries perceive the root causes, current consequences, and proposed solutions to worldwide challenges, *Global Viewpoints* volumes offer readers opportunities to enhance their global awareness and their knowledge of cultures worldwide.

Introduction

"The U.S. economy, once the envy of the world, is now viewed across the globe with suspicion. America has become shackled by an immovable mountain of debt that endangers its prosperity and threatens to bring the rest of the world economy crashing down with it."

—Hamid Varzi,
International Herald Tribune, *2007*

From 2008–2009, the world experienced what the International Monetary Fund (IMF) in its *2009 World Economic Outlook* called "by far the deepest global recession since the Great Depression." This economic downturn was sparked by a global financial crisis.

The crisis originated in the United States. During the 2000s, Americans began to invest heavily in houses. As more and more people purchased houses with borrowed money, the prices of houses rose and rose. This trend was partially fueled by low interest rates, which made it cheaper to borrow money. Thus, Dean Baker, writing in *Real-World Economics Review* in 2008, noted that "extraordinarily low interest rates accelerated the run-up in house prices."

Price inflation of this sort is often referred to as a "bubble." William Watson, writing in the *Gazette* in 2006, said that "A bubble . . . is a run-up in prices going beyond anything that reasonable economic calculation can justify." Watson added that "when enough people do finally recover their senses . . . [the] bubble bursts." This is what happened in the United States in 2007, and by the end of the year, the bubble had collapsed, and housing prices had dropped more than 15 percent.

During the bubble, banks had often lent money to people who were bad credit risks; these loans are known as subprime mortgages. The banks figured that as long as housing prices went up, they would always be able to recover their money, because even if a creditor defaulted, the house itself could always be sold for a profit. Based on this theory, banks repackaged and sold these mortgages as investments, or mortgage-based securities. Thus, an investor could buy a bunch of mortgages (or a small piece of a bunch of mortgages) which were guaranteed to pay back a certain return.

The banks were so sure that these mortgage-based securities would always pay that they even sold insurance on the investments. These insurance contracts were called credit default swaps. A credit default swap (CDS) means an investor in mortgage-based securities would pay a certain amount of money to the bank on a regular basis as long as the securities made money. If the securities ever stopped making money, though, the bank would have to pay the investor a large sum. CDSs were very popular because they made investors feel safer, and banks were certain they would never have to pay on them; investments would never default because housing prices would go up forever, or so they believed. As a result, as Janet Morrissey reported in *TIME* in 2009, "The CDS market exploded over the past decade to more than $45 trillion in mid-2007. . . . This is roughly twice the size of the U.S. stock market."

When the bubble burst and housing prices did start to go down, banks found themselves in a precarious position. Much of the banks' money was invested in mortgages that were now shown to be bad debts. To make matters worse, the banks had in many cases promised to pay other investors through credit default swaps if these loans went bad. The resulting strain caused a series of catastrophic failures of large banks in the United States. Bear Stearns, a large investment bank, first noted publicly that it was having trouble because of subprime loans in July 2007. On September 7, 2008, Fannie Mae (Federal National Mortgage Association) and Freddie Mac (Federal Home Loan Mortgage Corporation), the two largest mortgage lenders in the United States, had to be bailed out by the U.S. government. On September 15, 2008, Lehman Brothers, another large bank, declared bankruptcy. In the following weeks, Washington Mutual also collapsed. The U.S. government also stepped in to save the nation's largest insurance company, AIG. The rescue package was $85 billion.

The banking crisis was not confined to the United States. In the first place, other nations had their own housing bubbles. Even more important, banks and investors around the world had placed money in U.S. mortgages. As Jim Haughey wrote on the blog Market Insights, "Foreign investors were net buyers of about $20 billion a month of agency bonds throughout the 2004–05 housing boom and through mid-2008." Thus, foreign banks faced many of the same problems U.S. banks did when the U.S. housing bubble burst. As a result, in October 2007, the German government was forced to spend $50 billion to prop up the bank Hypo Real Estate. Around the same time, Iceland nationalized, or imposed government control of, the country's second largest bank. In February 2008, the British government also had to nationalize one of its major banks. The problem was not solely confined to Europe. Investors in Asia, especially in China, also held many U.S. assets.

The bank crisis has had a major impact on the world economy. Stock markets worldwide plunged; the U.S. Dow Jones average dropped to its lowest level since 1997. Britain's stock market was down by more than 5 percent at one point, while Japan's stock market fell by almost 4 percent.

Another impact of the financial storm has been a liquidity crisis. Liquidity is the ability to raise cash quickly. Many businesses rely on short-term borrowing to meet payroll or other obligations. But, as Chris Arnold noted in an October 2008 story for National Public Radio (NPR), "banks are already short of cash because of losses in the housing bust, so they're a lot less willing to lend money to everybody else." Without liquidity, many businesses can't function.

As businesses fail, unemployment rises and the economy spirals into a recession. This has had a devastating effect worldwide. The International Monetary Fund and the World Bank released a joint statement in April 2009 calling the recession "a human and development calamity" which "has already driven more than 50 million people into extreme poverty." The International Labour Organization predicted that 20 million jobs would be lost by the end of 2009. Increases in poverty and unemployment have also resulted in angry protests from Iceland to France to China. Jack Ewing, writing in *Business Week* in March 2009, noted that "global political instability is rising fast." Governments have responded in various ways to the crisis. As noted, some have bailed out or nationalized failing banks. Many nations have also put together stimulus packages to jump start the economy and create jobs. China announced a $586 billion stimulus plan in November 2008. The United States passed a $780 billion stimulus in February 2009; in the same month Germany passed a $63 billion package and Australia a $27 billion one.

In March 2009, Vikas Bajaj reported in the *New York Times* that the economy was turning around, or as he put it, "there was a sense among some economists and Wall Street analysts that if the bottom was not touched, perhaps the freefall was at least slowing." Stock markets seemed to be ticking upwards, and some banks were reporting profits again. Few are willing to predict whether the recovery will last or what the long term effects of the economic crisis will be. *Global Viewpoints: The Global Financial Crisis* addresses the causes of the crisis, the effects on wealthy and developing nations, and recommendations for the future.

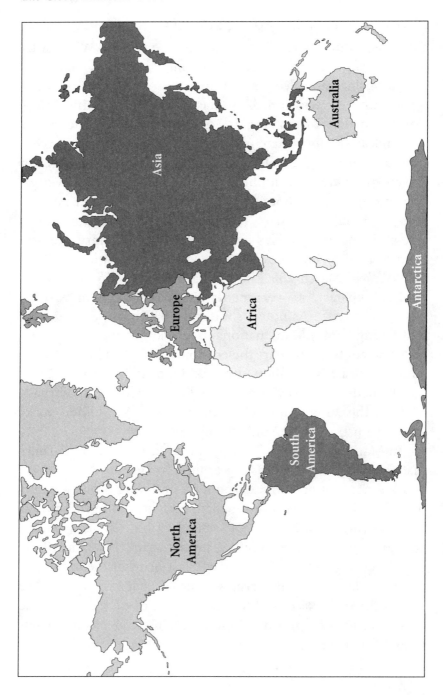

Causes of the Global Financial Crisis

China and Russia Blame U.S. Policies for the Crisis

Jenny Booth

Jenny Booth has written articles for the Times of London *and the* Sunday Times. *In this viewpoint, she reports that the leaders of China and Russia accused America of creating the economic crisis through greedy pursuit of profit, low savings rates, high consumption, and poor regulations. Booth asserts that China and Russia have suffered in the financial crisis, and there has been a lack of cooperation among these two powers and the United States to get the interdependent economy back on track.*

As you read, consider the following questions:

1. Who are the premiers of China and Russia?
2. According to Vladimir Putin, how long did it take investment banks to post losses exceeding the profits that they made in the last 25 years?
3. According to the International Monetary Fund, what is China's predicted growth rate for 2009?

The premiers of China and Russia accused America of sparking the economic crisis as the Davos [Switzerland] political and business summit made a gloomy start.

Wen Jiabao and Vladimir Putin [the premiers of China and Russia, respectively] both blamed "capitalist excesses" for

Jenny Booth, "China and Russia Blame US for Financial Crisis," *Times Online*, January 29, 2009. Copyright © 2009 Times Newspapers Ltd. Reproduced by permission.

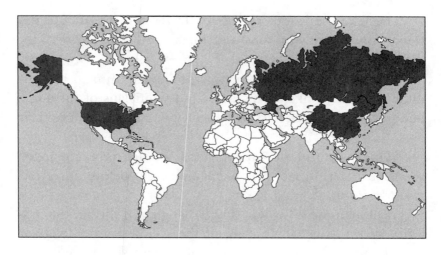

the global downturn, as one followed the other to the podium at the opening of the World Economic Forum last night [January 2009].

American Policies Were Reckless

The Chinese premier began with a speech asserting that the worst recession since the Great Depression had been caused by blind pursuit of profit.

In a thinly veiled attack on America, Mr. Wen blamed "inappropriate macroeconomic policies of some economies" and "prolonged low savings and high consumption".

> *The Chinese premier began with a speech asserting that the worst recession since the Great Depression had been caused by blind pursuit of profit.*

He blasted the "excessive expansion of financial institutions in blind pursuit of profit and the lack of self-discipline among financial institutions and ratings agencies", while the "failure" of regulators had allowed the spread of toxic derivatives.

The Chinese leader called for faster reform of international financial institutions and for a "new world order" for the economy.

Mr. Putin, the Russian premier, following him to the podium, accused bankers, regulators and politicians of turning a blind eye to the "perfect storm" that was building before their eyes.

"This pyramid of expectations would have collapsed sooner or later. In fact it is happening right before our eyes," said Mr. Putin.

"Although the crisis was simply hanging in the air, the majority strove to get their share of the pie, be it one dollar or one billion, and did not want to notice the rising wave."

Mr. Putin said that he would not criticise the United States, but then added: "I just want to remind you that just a year ago, American delegates speaking from this rostrum emphasised the US economy's fundamental stability and its cloudless prospects."

Condoleezza Rice, when US secretary of state, gave a speech in Davos last year [2008] saying the US economy was safe.

Mr. Putin went on: "Today investment banks, the pride of Wall Street, have virtually ceased to exist. In just 12 months they have posted losses exceeding the profits they made in the last 25 years. This example alone reflects the real situation better than any criticism.

"The existing financial system has failed. Sub-standard regulation has contributed to the crisis, failing to duly heed tremendous risks."

Cooperation Is Necessary

Mr. Wen said that the crisis had posed "severe challenges" for China, which has pursued a mirror image policy of investing heavily in the United States and buying up US debt, just as America was plunging deeper and deeper into the red.

Russia Is Drowning in Bad Debt

Russian banks' bad loans will quadruple to $70 billion this year [2009], deepening the country's worst financial crisis since the government's 1998 debt default, a Bloomberg survey shows.

Non-performing loans will increase to 12.8 percent of the 18.4 trillion rubles ($549 billion) owed by Russian companies and individuals by the end of this year....

The World Bank said last week that a "silent tsunami" of bad debt threatens to stall a recovery in Russia, the world's largest energy-exporting economy. The government may need to provide as much as $50 billion for bank bailouts.

Emma O'Brien and William Mauldin,
"Russia Bad Loans May Reach $70 Billion, Deepen Crisis,"
Bloomberg.com, April 9, 2009. www.bloomberg.com.

The effects of the downturn have hit Chinese jobs and overseas markets, causing some social unrest. Four million migrant Chinese workers have so far been thrown out of work.

Mr. Wen said that China now needed 8 percent growth in 2009 to maintain social stability, while the International Monetary Fund predicted 6.7 percent for this year.

Both Mr. Wen and Mr. Putin called for greater cooperation in international affairs from new US President Barack Obama—conspicuous by his absence from Davos, as he battles to get his $825 bn [billion] fiscal stimulus package through Congress.

The prospects for cooperation between the US and China have seemed to recede in recent days, after the new US Treasury Secretary Timothy Geithner last week revealed that Mr.

Obama believes China has been manipulating its currency, deliberately refusing to allow it to rise in value against the dollar in order to gain an edge in trade.

"In meeting the international financial crisis, it is imperative for the two countries to enhance cooperation; that is my message to the US administration," Mr. Wen said.

Both the Chinese and Russian premiers also spoke out against protectionism, and said that excessive government intervention would harm recovery prospects.

Trevor Manuel, South Africa's Finance Minister, described wealthy nations as adopting a "lemming-like approach, trying to get to the precipice without knowing what their money would buy".

[British prime minister] Gordon Brown, Chancellor Angela Merkel of Germany and the Japanese prime minister Taro Aso—who have between them spent hundreds of billions of dollars battling the crisis—were also among about 40 heads of state or government who will speak this week.

There were plenty of other critics among the record attendance at Davos of the bank recapitalisations and fiscal stimulus packages that wealthy countries have put in place to counter the crisis.

Trevor Manuel, South Africa's Finance Minister, described wealthy nations as adopting a "lemming-like approach, trying to get to the precipice without knowing what their money would buy".

The economic turmoil has overshadowed efforts to highlight other key issues at the conference, including climate change, conflicts around the world and poverty alleviation campaigns, but Ban Ki-moon, the UN [United Nations] Secretary General, was due to speak about the Gaza conflict [in which Israel launched a military campaign in the Gaza Strip in December 2008–January 2009] in Davos today.

The Greed of Financial Institutions Caused the Crisis

Oskari Juurikkala

Oskari Juurikkala is a Finnish economist and lawyer whose consulting firm, Ansgar Economics, advises on macroeconomics and investment strategies. He is the editor of Kultainfo.com, a financial Web site focusing on precious metals. In this viewpoint, Juurikkala says that financial instruments called derivatives have been used in unethical ways to fool regulators. He argues that while regulations would help, a moral transformation and a renunciation of greed is what is really needed.

As you read, consider the following questions:

1. According to Oskari Juurikkala, what are derivatives?
2. What act does Juurikkala explain was passed after Enron to create a new layer of regulations?
3. According to Juurikkala, what really destroyed Enron?

"Greed is good," insisted Gordon Gekko in the 1987 film *Wall Street*. Most of us disagree. Recent events in the mortgage lending industry prove us right.

The "subprime loan crisis" has been making headlines since it began in August [2007]. It refers to the fact that a relatively high percentage of mortgages offered to people with significant probability of default have gone sour.

The moniker is a bit misleading, though. The crisis we are witnessing starts from risky loan deals but will extend to all varieties of credit and risk: consumer loans, credit cards, businesses, and so on. It is just about to heat up but the roots of this crisis were laid years ago.

Derivatives Can Be Dangerous

It's a credit crisis, but credit per se is not the problem. The problem lies in how credit was traded from one hand to another on an unprecedented scale. This was done through financial innovations called derivatives.

Derivatives are contracts that allow companies to trade risks that derive from some other underlying assets. For example, a currency futures contract lets you . . . lock into a specific foreign exchange rate. It's a sensible move if you trade abroad and do not wish to carry the risk of a sudden change in exchange rates.

Recent decades brought much trickier—and riskier—derivatives, such as "over-the-counter credit default swaps (CDS)." Sound complex? It is.

Derivatives could . . . be used to circumvent regulations that protect investors and the public.

Credit derivatives permit lenders to transfer their credit risks (mortgage defaults) to third parties, such as hedge funds. Thus banks can do more business. In the 1990s and 2000s, credit derivatives became a massive global gamble.

If used properly, derivatives are useful and ethically unobjectionable. They enable efficient risk allocation that benefits all parties concerned. But their abuse is a nightmare. They become a house of cards, built on greed.

Derivatives could, for instance, be used to circumvent regulations that protect investors and the public. These stakeholders lack the time or ability to track the risks taken by companies, which is why financial institutions cannot freely

---

Increasing Regulations on Risk Trading

One corner of the wild and wooly world of derivatives is about to get a little tamer—and not a moment too soon for those who fret over the rising cost of bailouts.

The banks that handle the bulk of the trading in credit default swaps [CDS] . . . are adopting new trading and settlement rules this week [April 2009] in a shift the industry has labeled the 'big bang'. . .

The moves should eventually make it easier for regulators to oversee the CDS market, whose rapid growth and limited transparency have long been a source of acute anxiety.

Daily Times,
"Banks Brace for Derivatives 'Big Bang,'"
April 9, 2009. www.dailytimes.com.

---

invest in risky asset classes. But through derivatives, many institutions made complex speculative bets without regulators catching on.

If it works, it pays off. Companies make abnormal profits and managers take huge bonuses. If it doesn't work, someone else will usually pay the bill, such as investors and bank depositors.

Then there's the Fed [Federal Reserve System], always keen to save bankers by printing more money. The losers are the unsuspecting working and middle classes, whose savings are eroded by inflation. What to do?

How to Curtail Greed

One thing we need is better rules. True, we have lots of regulations in financial markets. Some are so complex that most professionals can't follow them. Often they are equally unhelpful.

Derivatives are a case in point. After Enron [an American energy company that went bankrupt amidst revelations of accounting fraud in 2001], we got the Sarbanes-Oxley Act, which costs fortunes to U.S.-listed companies. Despite this new layer of regulation, abuses are rampant: massive off-balance sheet items, shadowy over-the-counter deals, [financial contracts the prices of which are not readily or publicly available] unrealistic marking-to-model pricing [basing a price on a financial model rather than on the actual market price], murky offshore special purpose entities (SPEs) [a limited company created to shield a parent company from financial losses]. Risk-hiding has become widespread, often with the explicit or tacit approval of regulators.

We need simpler rules, ones that tackle the real issues. But more than rules, we need personal conversion.

Remember Enron? "They broke the law," people say. Well, yes. They also abused financial derivatives, SPEs and a range of other tricks to hide their excessive risks. But what really destroyed Enron, and made it so dangerous, was its corporate culture. It was infected with institutionalized greed.

The current situation is Enron writ large. We have more derivatives, more leverage [borrowing money to invest], and bigger losses. Wall Street is hardly superior when it comes to generosity and detachment from worldly goods.

We need simpler rules, ones that tackle the real issues. But more than rules, we need personal conversion.

The apostle Paul identified the issue 2,000 years ago: *the love of money is the root of all evils* (1 Timothy 6: 10). He concurred with Jesus, who said, *You cannot serve God and mammon* [wealth or greed personified] (Matthew 6: 24).

The goods of this world are good. But we have to pursue them in the right order, guided by love of God and neighbor. It applies to personal life and it applies to finance. Wisdom shuns greed. Prudence depends on the moral virtues, as Aristotle taught. Greed is like pride: it blinds.

2008 will be a tough year. We may witness the largest financial crisis in history. We need to study the past to see how we got here. But more than that, we must think about the future.

In order to make finance safe for our children, we need better laws and regulations. This is hard to accomplish, however, and it's never enough. Unless people—at least most people—are willing to do what is right *because it is right*, our laws will be objects of mockery and abuse.

First we need a change of heart. Perhaps we'll then get the laws right too.

"Boom Thinking" Caused the Crisis

Robert J. Shiller

Robert J. Shiller is a professor of economics at Yale University and an economics columnist for the New York Times. *In the following viewpoint, Shiller says that the boom in mortgage lending was fueled by a belief that housing prices would rise indefinitely. Shiller calls this belief a "social contagion"—an epidemic of a certain kind of thinking. Since people believe prices will go up, they spend more money, pushing prices further up, and convincing others to spend. Regulators and experts also tend to be caught up in the enthusiasm, creating a speculative bubble that can have complicated and disastrous effects.*

As you read, consider the following questions:

1. Between 1997 and 2005, how much did homeownership rates in the United States increase, according to the U.S. Census?

2. According to Robert J. Shiller, with whom did Alan Greenspan have an overly strong ideological alignment?

3. What was the federal funds rate between mid-2003 and mid-2004?

B y now the whole world has heard the story of the problems in the subprime mortgage [a housing loan for a person with poor credit history] market, which began to show up in the United States in 2007 and then spread to other countries. Home prices and homeownership had been booming since the late 1990s, and investing in a house had seemed a sure route to financial security and even wealth.

Homeownership Rates Boom

U.S. homeownership rates rose over the period 1997–2005 for all regions, all age groups, all racial groups, and all income groups. According to the U.S. Census, the homeownership rate increased from 65.7% to 68.9% (which represents an 11.5% increase in the number of owner-occupied homes) over that period. The increases in homeownership were largest in the West, for those under the age of 35, for those with below-median incomes, and for Hispanics and blacks.

Encouraging homeownership is a worthy and admirable national goal. It conveys a sense of participation and belonging, and high homeownership rates are beneficial to a healthy society. . . . But the subprime housing dilemma in the United States points to problems with overpromoting homeownership. Homeownership, for all its advantages, is not the ideal housing arrangement for all people in all circumstances. And we are now coming to appreciate the reality of this, for the homeownership rate has been falling in the United States since 2005.

The Boom Turns to Bust

What was the chain of events in the subprime crisis? Overly aggressive mortgage lenders, compliant appraisers, and complacent borrowers proliferated to feed the housing boom. Mortgage originators, who planned to sell off the mortgages to securitizers [people who would pool and repackage the loans] stopped worrying about repayment risk. They typically made only perfunctory efforts to assess borrowers' ability to repay their loans—often failing to verify borrowers' incomes with the Internal Revenue Service, even if they possessed signed authorization forms permitting them to do so. Sometimes these lenders enticed the naïve, with poor credit histories, to borrow in the ballooning subprime mortgage market. These mortgages were packaged, sold, and resold in sophisticated but arcane ways to investors around the world, setting the stage for a crisis of truly global proportions. The housing bubble, combined with the incentive system implicit in the securitization process, amplified moral hazard [the likelihood that a party insulated from risk will act in an unethical way], further emboldening some of the worst actors among mortgage lenders.

Overly aggressive mortgage lenders, compliant appraisers, and complacent borrowers proliferated to feed the housing boom.

High home prices made it profitable to build homes, and the share of residential investment in U.S. gross domestic product (GDP) rose to 6.3% in the fourth quarter of 2005, the highest level since the pre-Korean War housing boom of 1950–51. The huge supply of new homes began to glut the market, and, despite the optimistic outlooks of national leaders, U.S. home prices began to fall in mid-2006. As prices declined at an accelerating rate, the boom in home construction collapsed.

At the same time, mortgage rates began to reset to higher levels after initial "teaser" periods ended. Borrowers, particularly subprime borrowers, began defaulting, often owing more than their homes were worth or unable to support their higher monthly payments with current incomes. Now many of the financial institutions that participated in what once seemed a brave new world of expanding homeownership and exotic financial innovation are in varying degrees of distress. The world's credit markets have shown symptoms of locking up. . . .

Rising Prices Create "Boom Thinking"

While every historical event is the outcome of a combination of factors, I believe . . . that the most important single element to be reckoned with in understanding this or any other speculative boom is the *social contagion* of boom thinking, mediated by the common observation of rapidly rising prices. This social contagion lends increasing credibility to stories—I call them "new era" stories—that appear to justify the belief that the boom will continue. The operation of such a social contagion of ideas is hard to see because we do not observe the contagion directly, and it is easy to neglect its underlying causes.

Some observers seem to be ideologically opposed to the idea that contagion of thought patterns plays any role in our collective thinking. Indeed, people think the world is led by independent minds who invariably act with great intelligence. Since the bubble years of the late 1990s, intellectual arrogance of this kind appears to have exerted a growing influence over the world economy.

Alan Greenspan, [chairman of the Federal Reserve from 1987 to 2006] in a *Financial Times* op-ed piece in March 2008, recognized—well after the bubble was over—that there had indeed been "euphoria" and "speculative fever." But, he wrote, "The essential problem is that our models—both risk models and econometric models—as complex as they have become—are still too simple to capture the full array of governing variables that drive global economic reality. A model, of necessity, is an abstraction from the full detail of the real world."

Greenspan thus did eventually acknowledge the obvious reality of bubbles, but he never seemed to embrace the view that a good part of what drives people's thinking is purely social in nature. He espoused the idea that the mathematical econometric models of individual behavior are the only tools that we will ever have with which to understand the world, and that they are limited only by the amount and nature of our data and our ability to deal with complexity. He does not seem to respect research approaches from the fields of psychology or sociology.

Perhaps his lack of attention to bubbles reflected, at least in part, an overly strong ideological alignment with some of the views of his former mentor, the philosopher Ayn Rand. She idealized the strength of individual, independent, courageous action and rational selfish man as a "heroic being." But a tendency to base one's self-esteem on a belief in the possibility of economic success through individual action goes far beyond the admirers of Ayn Rand.

The changing zeitgeist drives common opinion among the members of society at any point in time and place, and this zeitgeist changes as new ideas gain prominence and recede in importance within the collective thinking.

Economists Do Not Understand Sociology

What seems to be absent from the thinking of many economists and economic commentators is an understanding that contagion of ideas is consistently a factor in human affairs. Just as there are interregional differences in matters of opinion (as evidenced, for example, by the geographic concentration of support for political parties), so too are there intertemporal differences. The changing zeitgeist [the general trend of thought at a given time] drives common opinion among the members of society at any point in time and place, and this zeitgeist changes as new ideas gain prominence and recede in importance within the collective thinking. Spec-

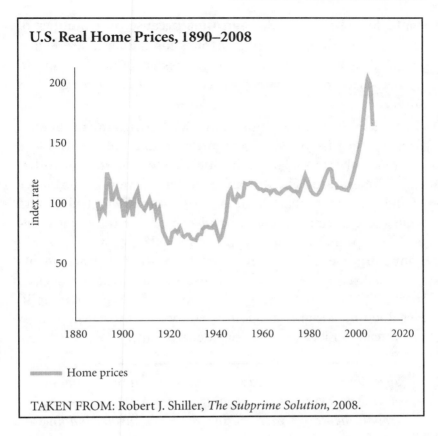

U.S. Real Home Prices, 1890–2008

index rate

200

150

100

50

1880   1900   1920   1940   1960   1980   2000   2020

▬▬▬ Home prices

TAKEN FROM: Robert J. Shiller, *The Subprime Solution*, 2008.

ulative markets are merely exceptionally good places in which to observe the ebb and flow of the zeitgeist.

Understanding such a social contagion is a lot like understanding a disease epidemic. Epidemics crop up from time to time, and their timing often baffles experts. But a mathematical theory of epidemiology has been developed, and it can help medical authorities better understand these apparently mysterious events.

Every disease has a contagion rate (the rate at which it is spread from person to person) and a removal rate (the rate at which individuals recover from or succumb to the illness and so are no longer contagious). If the contagion rate exceeds the removal rate by a necessary amount, an epidemic begins. The

37

contagion rate varies through time because of a number of factors. For example, contagion rates for influenza are higher in the winter, when lower temperatures encourage the spread of the virus in airborne droplets after infected individuals sneeze.

So it is in the economic and social environment. Sooner or later, some factor boosts the infection rate sufficiently above the removal rate for an optimistic view of the market to become widespread. There is an escalation in public knowledge of the arguments that would seem to support that view, and soon the epidemic spirals up and out of control. Almost everyone appears to think—if they notice at all that certain economic arguments are more in evidence—that the arguments are increasingly heard only because of their true intellectual merit. The idea that the prominence of the arguments is in fact due to a social contagion is hardly ever broached, at least not outside university sociology departments.

Speculative price increases encourage genuine economic optimism, hence more spending, hence greater economic growth, hence yet more optimism, hence further bidding up of prices.

"Boom Thinking" Creates Feedback Loops

In the recent speculative housing boom, an optimistic view of the market was certainly much in evidence. In a survey that [economist] Karl Case and I conducted in 2005, when the market was booming, we found that the median expected price increase among San Francisco home buyers over the next ten years was 9% a year, and the mean expected price increase was 14% a year. About a third of the respondents reported truly extravagant expectations—occasionally over 50% a year. On what did they base such outlooks? They had observed significant price increases and heard others' interpretation of such increases. We were witnessing the contagion of an interpretation or a way of forming expectations.

An important part of what happens during a speculative bubble is mediated by the marketplace, to which many people are attentive, and by the prices that are observed there and subsequently amplified by the news media. What do we mean by "amplified" in this context? The media weave stories around price movements, and when those movements are upward, the media tend to embellish and legitimize "new era" stories with extra attention and detail. Feedback loops appear, as price increases encourage belief in "new era" stories, promote the contagion of those stories, and so lead to further price increases. The price-story-price loop repeats again and again during a speculative bubble.

The feedback loops also take the form of price-economic activity-price loops. Speculative price increases encourage genuine economic optimism, hence more spending, hence greater economic growth, hence yet more optimism, hence further bidding up of prices. Most persons can be forgiven for not seeing that the sense of economic prosperity that usually attends a major speculative bubble is actually caused by the bubble itself and not by economic fundamentals.

People Trust the Group

Under certain circumstances the explanations for contagion and feedback during speculative bubbles may be perfectly rational, and "rational bubbles" can be part of the story. A number of economic theorists have discussed the possibility of such bubbles.

The essential element of these rational bubble theories is that people may learn about the information that others have by observing their behavior. They cannot respond directly to the information that others have, since they cannot see inside their heads. But they may base their own decisions on the *actions* of others (as when they bid up speculative prices), which they interpret, wholly rationally, as reflecting valid information about economic fundamentals.

The problem is that we can arrive at a situation in which people are generally adopting an excessively optimistic (or excessively pessimistic) view, because they are rationally but mistakenly judging the information that others have. To borrow a term used by economic theorists Sushil Bikhchandani, David Hirshleifer, and Ivo Welch, speculative bubbles may be caused by "information cascades." An information cascade occurs when those in a group disregard their own independent, individually collected information (which might otherwise encourage them *not* to subscribe to a boom or other mass belief) because they feel that everyone else simply couldn't be wrong. And when they disregard their own independent information, and act instead on general information as they perceive it, they squelch their own information. It is no longer available to the group and so does not figure in further collective judgments. Thus, over time, the quality of group information declines.

Psychological, epidemiological, and economic theory all point to an environment in which feedback of enthusiasm for speculative assets, or feedback of price increases into further price increases, can be expected to produce speculative bubbles from time to time. They make it clear that these bubbles can have complicated—sometimes random and unpredictable—dynamics.

Experts and Regulators Catch the Contagion

The interpretation of the bubble that I have just offered is not the conventional wisdom. Other factors are widely cited as the cause of the housing boom. I argue here that, to a large extent, these other factors were themselves substantially a *product* of the bubble, and not exogenous factors that caused the bubble.

The U.S. Federal Reserve [the central banking system of the United States] cut its key rate, the federal funds rate [the interest rate banks charge each other for loans], to 1% in mid-2003 and held it there until mid-2004, roughly the period of most rapid home-price increase. Moreover, the real (inflation-corrected) federal funds rate was negative for thirty-one months, from October 2002 to April 2005, an interval again centered on the most rapid rise in home prices. Since 1950 the only other period of low rates as long as this one was the thirty-seven-month interval from September 1974 to September 1977.

We should not, however, view this period of very loose monetary policy as an *exogenous* cause of the bubble. For the monetary policy—both that of the Fed and that of other central banks around the world—was driven by economic conditions that were created by the bursting of the stock market bubble of the 1990s, and the real estate boom was itself in some ways a repercussion of that same stock market bubble.

The monetary policy appears to have been driven at least in part by the same lack of understanding that produced the bubble itself.

This loose policy would not have been implemented if Alan Greenspan and others involved with monetary policy had comprehended that we were going through a housing bubble that would burst. Thus the monetary policy appears to have been driven at least in part by the same lack of understanding that produced the bubble itself. The Fed was excessively focused on preventing recession and deflation because they honestly saw the home-price increases as continuing—if at a reduced pace—indefinitely, even if they were to implement a monetary policy that would feed the bubble.

The Weakness of Banking Regulations Caused the Crisis

Vince Cable

Vince Cable, economic spokesman for the Liberal Democrats, is the author of The Storm: The World Economic Crisis and What It Means. *In the following viewpoint, Cable discusses various options that are available for fixing the banking industry in the United Kingdom (UK). Certain UK banks are considered "too big to fail" and they want to retain their investment banking wings, but these pose a great financial risk to the taxpayer; therefore, the author favors either tighter government regulation of them or less government protection for them. Cable suggests that lack of regulation as well as the inability of regulators to monitor financial activity effectively were failures of the banking system revealed by the financial crisis. The author contends that further regulation is necessary to protect the wider UK economy from the financial risks undertaken by banks beyond the borders of the UK and that legislators should not let complaints of suppression of innovation and competitiveness lead them to give in to the banks and so put the UK economy at risk.*

As you read, consider the following questions:

1. According to Cable, what is the effect of political scandal on the attitude of bankers in regard to the solution of the financial crisis?

Vince Cable, "The Bankers Cannot Believe Their Luck: The Disgrace of the Political Class Has Become Their Salvation. And Lax Regulation Has Left Taxpayers Vulnerable to the Irresponsible Excesses of the Greedy Money Men. This Is What Must Now Be Done ...," *New Statesman*, vol. 138, no. 4955, June 29, 2009, pp. 22–25. Copyright © 2009 New Statesman, Ltd. Reproduced by permission.

2. According to Cable, what did the government in the UK do to rescue the banks in the financial crisis?

3. According to Cable, who is leading the new regulatory agenda that the author hopes will reduce or spread the risk of large banks?

Until the drama over MPs' expenses, workers in the financial services had been reeling from a succession of blows: collapsing banks, nationalisations, frozen bonuses, job losses and contemptuous, withering condemnation by the public and by opinion-formers in the media, church pulpits and parliament. An optimistic scenario was one of slow rehabilitation under a less permissive regime involving tougher regulation, partial public ownership of banks and a diminished, chastened City.

Now the bankers can't believe their luck. A couple of days after the first revelations in the *Daily Telegraph*, the headline in the City's free newspaper *City AM* was a shout of orgasmic release: "Now THEY can't lecture US." It said it all. Collapse of moral authority and politicians' will. Back to business as usual.

The dangers of drift were highlighted in the speech given at Mansion House on 17 June by Mervyn King, governor of the Bank of England. He publicly expressed discomfort at the idea of banks that are "too big to fail": he has concluded that such banks are simply too big. But the government is reluctant to tackle these banks, as the conduct of Lord Myners and the institutionalised passivity of UK Financial Investments Ltd (UKFI)—the Treasury-backed bank shareholder body—indicates. Instead, there seems to be a yearning to disengage government from the financial sector as quickly as possible. Political developments have made that disengagement easier to achieve, now that parliamentarians, including members of the Treasury select committee, have been collectively discredited, and power within the Labour government has shifted from a wounded Prime Minister to a revitalised Chancellor articulating the Treasury line.

It is deeply worrying that some of the most important policy questions for a generation are now being decided by default and in a political vacuum. How can a semi-nationalised banking system best serve the different but overlapping interests of UK bank borrowers, depositors and taxpayers, as well as private shareholders and bank executives? How should the systemic risks of banking—and the City generally—be managed through regulation, in order to safeguard the wider UK economy? Most important, is it actually possible for the UK to play host to a major financial service sector?

The bankers' view is that UK politicians need to get off their backs as quickly as possible and get the banks back into the private sector. . . .

The response to all these questions is a lazy, uncritical, self-serving one: that, bar a few regulatory tweaks that will need to be made, the previous regime was essentially fine. The bankers' view is that UK politicians need to get off their backs as quickly as possible and get the banks back into the private sector; to reverse "penal" (ie, 50 per cent) marginal tax rates; and to stop the European Commission, or more self-confident UK regulators, from "undermining the City's competitiveness". These arguments are winning. Indeed, there is a danger that the counter-revolution could soon become a rout.

Yet it is only a matter of months since half of the British banking system collapsed and had to be rescued by the state . . . through total or partial nationalisation. Thanks to that intervention, the banks have stabilised (if nothing more). Several small banks are now fully nationalised; RBS and the Lloyds Banking Group are partly nationalised; the two remaining global banks (HSBC and Barclays), along with the remainder of the sector, depend on a variety of implicit or explicit guarantees.

How we got to that point has been discussed elsewhere (including in my book *The Storm*): I am now concerned with the future. There is a bifurcation of paths opening up. One route builds on the experience of recent bank crises in Scandinavia, Israel, Korea and elsewhere, including the US, whose so-called Resolution Trust model helped to limit the savings and loans crisis of the late 1980s and early 1990s. Following this route, the state leads and manages a clean-up and restructuring of banks, usually within a decade or so. Approaches have varied, but there are some common elements: the wiping clean of the slate, in respect of losses incurred by existing private shareholders and the removal of failed management; fresh, taxpayer equity capital; structures to ensure that lending can continue unhindered to good, solvent borrowers; the valuation and active management of "bad" assets, in order to retrieve whatever value is left; then, in due course, the selling off of some or all publicly owned banks to achieve maximum return to the taxpayer and leave a varied ecology of properly regulated national banking institutions.

Some of us thought that was where the government was originally heading. After the October rescue, there were some tough-sounding conditions on new lending and curbing bonuses and, for a while, as it basked in the glow of international approval, the government seemed to be on the right track.

But it has gradually become apparent that we are being taken down a different route, where government money and guarantees are used to facilitate a quick return to "business as usual". UKFI has been populated by financiers rather than business people with experience as bank customers. The public-sector shareholders seem to have had no quarrel with bank management's efforts to build profitability and deleverage as quickly as possible.

The Asset Protection Scheme introduced in January also provides insurance cover for "toxic assets", which means the government has taken on an open-ended risk without a corresponding "upside" for the taxpayer. This route was chosen in preference to fresh government equity capital precisely because it makes a quick return to private-sector ownership easier. There is now a danger of premature reprivatisation, which would leave the taxpayer with a vast toxic dump of losses and a poor price for the share sale. There are already rumours that Northern Rock is being lined up for a rapid sale.

If banks are to return to "normal" commercial operation under private ownership, the issue arises of how they should be regulated. The Cruickshank report on banking, commissioned by Gordon Brown a decade ago, posed the central question: why should banks be allowed to pursue the maximisation of shareholder value—and management bonuses—when they are underwritten by the taxpayer? This question has never been answered properly. Banks should either surrender their protection and compete like other firms, or be protected and have their profit regulated like utilities. In the wake of a banking crisis, the logic is even starker. In the past few weeks we have seen leading executives at Barclays awarding themselves millions while the bank ultimately remains dependent on government guarantees, despite its precarious independence. It is not surprising that executives of the semi-nationalised banks want to follow suit.

What has brought the issue to a head is the judgement that the major UK-based banks are "too big to fail" and have to be rescued in a financial emergency. This concept is an economic and democratic outrage. Either they must be subject to tight state control or they should be broken up so that they are not "too big to fail". The point has been grasped, improbably, by ministers in banker-friendly countries such as Switzerland, and by our own central bank's governor. Yet ministers today seem no less terrified of confronting the banks than when Brown initially fled the battlefield a decade ago.

Change in UK Regulations Contributed to the Crisis

In 1997 Mr. [Gordon] Brown, then chancellor of the exchequer [minister in charge of finance], took bank supervision from the Bank of England and gave it to a new creation, the FSA [Financial Services Authority] with a view to integrating the oversight of increasingly diversified financial firms. The central bank retained theoretical responsibility for the stability of the financial sector, but few tools to secure it. . . .

Whether it was the policies or the personalities that were wrong, the system didn't work.

Economist, *"Bolting the Stable Door,"*
March 19, 2009. www.economist.com.

One solution would be to restrict protection, including deposit protection, to "narrow banks", confined to lending out no more than they receive in deposits. Other banks would operate competitively but be stripped of any protection. I, for one, am attracted to the concept; but it would involve a revolutionary change, a discontinuation of fractional banking altogether, and in the short run it is unlikely to be adopted.

A less drastic way of dealing with overgrown banks would be to split off the investment banking arms of the main global banks—what Mervyn King calls the "casinos"—and to confine government protection to the remaining "traditional" banking wings. These would then operate as regulated utilities: the model that broadly prevailed in the United States before the repeal of the Glass-Steagall Act a decade ago. The urgent need to change our system is highlighted by the ambition of Barclays Capital to become "the premier global investment bank": it is madness for the British taxpayer to be a last-resort guarantor for this kind of business. To be sure, the demarcation is not clear-cut: there is high-risk "traditional" banking and low-risk investment banking, and the separation of roles would not be straightforward. The big banks—HSBC and Barclays—argue that they would be stopped from tapping into the securitisation markets (which may, after recent disasters, not be quite the loss they believe it to be). There is also the implied threat that global banking operations will be withdrawn from the UK.

The government must face down this kind of blackmail. The British taxpayer simply should not be made responsible for the risks that global banks take outside our regulatory jurisdiction. There are undoubtedly technical difficulties in separating out those aspects of global banks that the government can guarantee and those it cannot, but these problems cannot be an excuse for bottling out completely.

One lesson of the financial crisis is that the "light-touch" regulatory approach was a failure. It may have failed in part because of the poor quality of bank supervision rather than the absence of regulation. And the rapid innovation of capital markets undoubtedly ran ahead of regulators' capacity to monitor activity effectively. But the vast cost to the British taxpayer—and the wider economy—of the banks' failure and the consequent bailout make it imperative that regulation be strengthened.

We are now at a crunch point. The need to strengthen and update the regulatory regime has collided with the financial institutions' growing confidence that they can keep the state off their backs. Self-serving arguments are being employed, notably that regulation will suppress "innovation". It will. It should. We need more financial "innovation" like a hole in the head.

The other argument is that regulation (and 50 per cent tax rates) will undermine the City's "competitiveness" and "drive away" banking and non-bank financial institutions. This argument has to be met head-on; the idea of a regulatory race to the bottom does not square with political and economic reality. Co-operation rather than regulatory arbitrage between the main jurisdictions will always be best, but if that cooperation does not materialise, the UK should not chase business by offering low standards that create wider risks for the UK economy. The arguments about City "competitiveness" are bogus, self-serving and dangerous. It is profoundly to be hoped that Brown, Alistair Darling, Ed Balls and others who fell for them so haplessly in the past have now learned their lesson.

The new regulatory agenda espoused by Lord Turner, chairman of the Financial Services Authority, is sensible and not especially controversial. Indeed, many in the City see it as a minor irritation, followed by a green light to get back to businesses "normal". It contains sensible elements—such as "macro prudential regulation" that would focus on systemic risks, rather than regulation of individual banks—and more controversial but basically prudent ideas, such as limiting loan-to-value ratios and/or multiples of income for mortgage lending.

Lord Turner has also supported the argument that the most dangerous forms of risk-taking in banking institutions can be limited by paying bonuses not in cash but in stock, redeemable after a period of years. As stock prices are depressed and the capital gains tax payable is only 18 per cent, any half-sober City trader will have worked out he should be doing this in any event. But it is not a silver bullet—the bosses at both Lehman Brothers and Bear Stearns had huge equity-related incentives, and look where they are today. These issues require pause for thought: there are bigger regulatory battles shaping up.

One concerns the proposal to establish a clearing house for complex financial derivatives so that they can be traded, netted and regulated. Properly regulated, these activities can spread risk and, in a general sense, add to stability. What is much more dangerous, as the recent financial crisis has illustrated, is to have a vast pyramid of paper claims—as in the CDS/CDO (credit default swap/collateralised debt obligation) "markets"—which cannot be settled in an orderly way through a clearing house. Important lessons can be learned from the recent collapse of General Motors. CDS contracts with a value in excess of \$35bn were netted down to \$2.2bn, causing little more than a ripple in the overall CDS market. The danger is that nothing will be done, setting up a huge systemic risk—and the next big crash.

One practical remedy would be to establish a clearing-house system as soon as possible. Big banks that make a lot of money from OTC ("over-the-counter") trading are not happy: if they were forced to use a regulated exchange they would lose this business. In practice, complex, structured derivatives would therefore be prevented. A second issue is whether the London Stock Exchange—and the Bank of England as the lender of last resort—are big and strong enough to support a clearing house dealing with transactions valued at many times the size of the world economy. Co-operation with the US is potentially important. And perhaps a European approach is required, in order to draw on the bigger firepower of the European Central Bank, but that may unleash some dangerous political demons.

But a more relaxed view is that there is a role for specialist financiers who pursue high yield via high risk—provided they do not depend on taxpayers' guarantees or indirectly contribute to the systemic risk that taxpayers underwrite.

Meanwhile, the European Union has precipitated another major regulatory battle by putting forward proposals, both for strengthening European co-operation over bank supervision—reluctantly conceded to by the UK—and for toughening the regulation of hedge funds and private equity. Britain's financial community has a collective paranoia about Europe, and there is envy of London's currently predominant role and a distaste for the freewheeling "Anglo-Saxon" model (not that German, Dutch or even French banks behaved very differently in the crisis).

However, it is surely eminently sensible to ask, as the European Commission is doing, whether these new forms of financial intermediation are healthy and adequately regulated. There are some critics who question the value of hedge funds altogether and would be happy to see them regulated out of existence. But a more relaxed view is that there is a role for specialist financiers who pursue high yield via high risk— provided they do not depend on taxpayers' guarantees or indirectly contribute to the systemic risk that taxpayers underwrite. The former has not been a problem in the recent crisis (no hedge fund has asked for government help), but the latter undoubtedly is. There is a proper debate to be had as to how hedge funds should be regulated: to treat the tentative proposals of the European Commission as akin to a Napoleonic invasion threat is simply idiotic.

There is a more fundamental argument about the scale of Britain's financial services industry in relation to the UK economy. I wouldn't expect the City to vote for contraction, or for curbs on its freedom to operate, any more than I would expect turkeys to vote for Christmas. But the poultry farmer— the Labour government—cannot just ask the turkeys what they want. He has to be willing to wield a knife and cut some throats. A combination of national, European and global regulation is necessary to ensure that the vast negative externalities associated with the City do not exceed the (genuine) benefits that the UK economy derives from a successful, internationally traded, financial services sector. In addition, there will have to be a major structural adjustment out of traded financial services into other services and manufacturing.

Unfortunately a weak, demoralised, delegitimised Labour government is in no shape to face this challenge, and a Tory government pumped up by City donations would have no need or inclination to take it on. The opportunity for reform and renewal is passing us by and, if it does, financial crises will return with even greater ferocity in years to come.

Low Interest Rates Caused the Crisis

Tito Boeri and Luigi Guiso

Tito Boeri is a professor of economics at Bocconi University in Milan, Italy. Luigi Guiso is a professor of economics at the European University Institute in Florence, Italy. In the following viewpoint, the authors argue that Alan Greenspan, former chairman of the Federal Reserve, made the wrong decision in drastically lowering interest rates in response to the recession of 2001. As a result, institutions and individuals were encouraged to take on excess risk and excess debt, resulting in the global financial crisis. The authors argue that in order to preserve financial stability, it is important not to cut interest rates too quickly in the current crisis.

As you read, consider the following questions:

1. According to Tito Boeri and Luigi Guiso, how much resemblance does the present crisis bear to the Great Depression?

2. According to Boeri and Guiso, is financial literacy low only in financially backward countries?

3. According to Boeri and Guiso, did the European Central Bank (ECB) lower interest rates as drastically as Alan Greenspan did?

It's difficult to predict how long the crisis in the world's financial markets will last. Its dynamics recall that of previous crises, such as that of 1998 (the Russian default and the collapse of LTCM [a US investment fund that failed in the late 1990s]) which have by now been forgotten by many. An excess of liquidity (i.e., an abundance of loans at low cost) has suddenly been transformed into a dearth of liquidity; many dealers find it hard to sell the assets in their portfolios. The present crisis bears little resemblance to the 1929 Great Depression, contrary to what some politicians and commentators assert. Fortunately Fed [US Federal Reserve chairman] ... Ben Bernanke has studied the Great Depression in depth. According to the analysis he did as an academic, the "Great Depression" was unleashed by a collapse of production and consumption, amplified by a drastic reduction in the supply of bank credit which came about largely because the Fed failed to act as a lender of last resort. Exactly the opposite is happening today. The world economy continues to grow at sustained rates since central banks have so far fulfilled their roles of supplying the necessary liquidity to the market. The only (perhaps nonnegligible) aspect that the current crisis shares with the Great Depression is that its epicenter is the US.

The Three Causes of the Crisis

It's useful to disentangle the causes of the crisis. Three factors contribute to the current crisis that was triggered by the expectation of defaults on subprime mortgages [housing loans made to those with poor credit] in the US:

- The low financial literacy of US households;

- The financial innovation that has resulted in the massive securitisation [pooling and repackaging] of illiquid assets; and

- The low interest rate policy followed by Alan Greenspan's Fed from 2001 to 2004. The third cause is by far the most important. Without Greenspan's policy, the present crisis probably would have never occurred.

The low borrowing rates for both short- and long-term maturity attracted throngs of borrowers—families above all who were seduced by the possibility of acquiring assets that had always been beyond their means.

The first ingredient of the crisis is a blend of bad information, financial inexperience and myopia of consumers/investors. They fell for the prospect of getting a mortgage at rates never seen before and then extrapolating these rates out for thirty years. This myopia was encouraged and indeed exploited by banks and other lenders eager to attract and retain clients. This is surprisingly similar to what has been seen in the past when banks and intermediaries have advised their clients to invest in financial assets ill-suited to their ability to bear risk. In both cases, a biased advisor is the reflection of a clear conflict of interest in the financial industry. Financial literacy is low not only in financially backward countries (as one would expect), but also in the US. Only two out of three Americans are familiar with the law of compound interest; less than half know how to measure the effects of inflation on the costs of indebtedness. Financial literacy is particularly low among those who have taken out subprime mortgages. The intermediaries exploited this financial illiteracy.

The second ingredient is the pace of financial innovation during the last ten years and the securitisation that it produced. Today it is easy to "liquidify" a portfolio of illiquid credits (typically a combination of bank loans or mortgages) so they can be packaged into investor portfolios [that is, it is possible to take an asset that cannot be easily exchanged such as a mortgage and repackage it so it can be traded]. Any bank with distressed loans has used this technique to securitise its own credits. Like all financial innovations, this too has pros

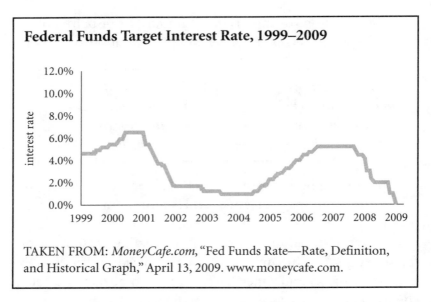

Federal Funds Target Interest Rate, 1999–2009

TAKEN FROM: *MoneyCafe.com*, "Fed Funds Rate—Rate, Definition, and Historical Graph," April 13, 2009. www.moneycafe.com.

and cons. The advantage is that by making an illiquid credit liquid, one can achieve important efficiency gains; investors can take longer-term positions and so earn a higher return. It also spreads the risk of insolvency across a much wider group, reducing the level of risk exposure of any individual agent. But securitisations also have their disadvantages. They weaken the incentives of financial intermediaries to monitor the behavior of the original borrower. In addition, since a credit that has become risky can be liquidated more easily, banks have less incentive to screen borrowers carefully. This opens the credit-markets doors to poor quality borrowers.

Greenspan Fueled Risky Behavior

The first two factors aren't new. Without the third factor—the legacy of the "central banker of the century"—the crisis probably would have never occurred. The monetary policy of low interest rates—introduced by Alan Greenspan [chairman of the Federal Reserve from 1987 to 2006] in response to the post-9/11 recession and the collapse of the new economy "bubble" [a speculative bubble involving Internet and tech stocks]—injected an enormous amount of liquidity into the global monetary system. This reduced short-term interest rates to 1%—their lowest level in 50 years. What's more, Greenspan spent the next two years maintaining interest rates at levels significantly below equilibrium. Interest rates were kept at low levels for a long time, and were often negative in inflation-adjusted terms. The result was no surprise. Low returns on traditional investments pushed investors and lenders to take bigger risks to get better returns. Financial intermediaries, in search of profits, extended credit to families and companies with limited financial strength. Investors with varying degrees of expertise duly reallocated their portfolios towards more lucrative but riskier assets in an attempt to increase their wealth and preserve its purchasing power. The low borrowing rates for both short- and long-term maturity attracted throngs of borrowers—families above all who were seduced by the possibility of acquiring assets that had always been beyond their means. At the same time, house prices soared, ultimately encouraging the additional extension of credit; the value of real estate seemed almost guaranteed.

We should not overreact, as has been done so many times in the past, by sowing the seeds of a future crisis today.

Thanks Alan! Today we're paying the cost of your overreaction to the 2001 recession. The ECB [European Central Bank] was wisely prudent and only let itself be partially tempted by Keynesian arguments [named for John Maynard Keynes] for reduced interest rates (which were already absurdly low) as a tool for attacking European stagnation. Many would like the ECB to lower rates now, arguing that to avoid a new "Great Depression" Europe needs Keynesian policy of the type followed in the USA, Great Britain and Germany after the 1929 collapse.

Moderate Policies Are Best

We think it is far better to avoid repeating Greenspan's error, and to avoid monetary policies that are too accommodating for too long. At present, central banks are acting correctly by injecting liquidity into the system. In such crises, one must be afraid of fear. Expectations can unleash downward spirals that make the most pessimistic prophecies come true. In addition, the market crisis hits everyone indiscriminately—even those who did not make money by extending mortgages too readily. Last Friday's [August 2007] press release of the Federal Open Market Committee didn't clarify whether half-point cut in the discount rate [an important interest rate] was intended to merely prevent a downward expectations spiral or whether it was the prelude to yet another overreaction to the market crisis. It's important to show soon that the lesson of Greenspan's error has been learned. We should not overreact, as has been done so many times in the past, by sowing the seeds of a future crisis today.

Abandoning the Gold Standard Caused the Crisis

Dominic Lawson

Dominic Lawson is a British journalist. In the following viewpoint, he discusses the work of economist Ludwig von Mises, who argued that unless a currency was tied to gold, politicians would be tempted to print money for short-term gain. Lawson suggests that when the United States went off the gold standard in the early 70s, it paved the way for a dangerous boom/bust cycle. Lawson argues that the instable currency and the tendency of governments to extend credit too easily may be at the root of the present crisis.

As you read, consider the following questions:

1. According to economist Liam Halligan, what is Britain's true level of national debt?
2. Which U.S. president does Dominic Lawson assert abandoned the gold standard in the midst of Vietnam War debt?
3. As Lawson reports, was the U.S. unemployment rate lower in January 1938 than it had been in September 1931?

My nearby market town of Lewes has started issuing its own pound notes: Tom Paine's portrait is on one side, Lewes Castle on the other. The Bullion Vault, a London gold broker, reports "phenomenal interest" in its product. The multi-millionaire media magnate Felix Dennis tells the *FT* that he has followed the instructions of his financial adviser to "buy gold. Physical bits, small bits, so when you need to get a sandwich you can take it down the shop and take 300 sandwiches away; God help me, in a vault here in London, I have huge quantities of small bits of gold."

We should not assume from this that the pound sterling is about to go the way of the Zimbabwean dollar. Lewes has ever been a contrary place; the Bullion Vault is obviously talking up its own business; Felix Dennis is highly impulsive.

Yet these are also straws in the wind, or rather a howling gale. When Governments spend vast sums of money to shore up the banking system, you just know that it would be all too convenient for it to let inflation erode the national debt incurred in the process. Even before these gigantic expenditures, Britain's true level of national debt, according to the economist Liam Halligan—the Government won't give the real figure including off-balance sheet liabilities—is over £1,300bn. This is equivalent to £50,000 per household. Perhaps Gordon Brown might call it "imprudence with a purpose"—he dumped Prudence some time ago, although he kept on telling everyone that they were still an item.

[Economist] Mises declared that the corruption and distortion of money by the state and bankers, usually to pay for wars, was the principal cause both of inflation and . . . boom and bust.

In America, the situation is much the same, only, as you would expect, bigger. Last Saturday, the digital display in New York showing the current level of national debt did not have enough digits to show the real number, after it breached the $10 trillion mark ($10,150,603,734,720 to be precise). Per American household this works out as $86,023

(£49,747); so Mr. Brown, in this respect at least, is in no position to lecture George W. Bush on economics.

There is, however, a small band of men and women—long insulted as fanatics or even fantasists by the political mainstream—who can now say: "We told you so." I am not referring to the Communist Party of Great Britain (Marxist-Leninist). No, I'm talking about the followers of the great Austrian economist Ludwig von Mises (1881–1973). In his 1912 work, *The Theory of Money and Credit*, Mises declared that the corruption and distortion of money by the state and bankers, usually to pay for wars, was the principal cause both of inflation and—to coin a phrase—boom and bust.

Mises believed that any currency which was not backed by gold was powerless to resist the depredations of governments and bankers addicted to the possibilities of limitless credit.

As the chief economic advisor to the Austrian government in the 1920s, Mises put his theories into practice and slowed down inflation in his native country (which, as a Jew, he later fled). He used his "cycle" theory to forecast that the "New Era" of apparently permanent prosperity in the 1920s was illusory, and that it would end in runs on banks and depression: The Wall Street crash of 1929 was exactly what Mises had predicted.

Mises believed that any currency which was not backed by gold was powerless to resist the depredations of governments and bankers addicted to the possibilities of limitless credit. Until the past few weeks, this has been seen as a bizarrely old-fashioned and eccentric outlook; but I would not be surprised if many young people—who have hitherto been comfortable with the idea of money as something which can just exist in the ether, travelling through the digital highway—now wonder whether anything of intrinsic value lies behind it all.

The Gold Standard Will Not Stabilize the Economy

A gold standard only works when everybody believes in the overall fiscal and monetary responsibility of the major world governments and the relative price of gold is fairly stable. . . . Saying you're on a gold standard does not suddenly make you credible. But it does set you up for some ferocious problems if people still doubt whether you've set your house in order.

James Hamilton,
"The Gold Standard and the Great Depression,"
Econbrowser.com, December 12, 2005. www.econbrowser.com.

As far as Mises was concerned, even money made of paper, if it had nothing behind it other than the good word of politicians and central bankers, was inherently unsound; he lived just long enough to see the United States of America—where he ended his days—break decisively with the international Gold Standard.

Up until August 1971, the owner of dollars could, at least theoretically, exchange them for gold. That month France, to whom the US owed about $3bn as part of the financing of the Vietnam War, demanded that the dollar debt be repaid in gold. Unfortunately, there was no longer enough in the vaults of Fort Knox. Apparently there exists a tape of Richard Nixon saying: "Screw the French!"—some accounts have the President using a more alliterative verb. America immediately came off the gold standard after which there was no theoretical limit to its ability to print money and—according to the followers of Mises—the age of high inflation was under way.

John Maynard Keynes, rather than Ludwig von Mises, is the economist whose name is currently being invoked on the airwaves in Britain. In his own day, too, Keynes obliterated Mises: it became fashionable to believe that Roosevelt's New Deal was a kind of successful rudimentary application of Keynesianism.

Yet Roosevelt's policy of massive intervention by the state to prop up wage rates and inflate credit gets a much better press than it ever deserved. Consider this: in September 1931 the US unemployment rate was 17.4 percent and the Dow Jones Industrial Average stood at 140. By January 1938, unemployment was still at 17.4 percent, and the Dow Average had dropped to 121.

Mises' followers insist that the present problems in the economies of the West have not been caused by laissez-faire, but by the opposite: politically sensitive central bankers so desperate to prevent any stock market slump that they cut interest rates to a level which turbo-charged the debt markets. So when George Osborne, as he did yesterday, declares that "laissez-faire is dead", the Mises-ites—one of whom is the libertarian ex-presidential candidate, Congressman Ron Paul— would protest that such a policy was never tried in the first place.

Yesterday, I spoke to one of the leading academic figures in that movement, Professor Thorsten Polleit of the Frankfurt School of Finance. The professor is less enthusiastic than the stock market about the British Government's injection of taxpayers' money into the weakest banks. He points out that by standing behind those banks, but giving no general guarantees, the government is encouraging savers to pull all their money out of well-run smaller institutions and switch it into badly run bigger banks.

The government will insist that it is no time to be debating economic theories and the origins of this crisis—that we should simply do what we can to inject confidence back into the system. Professor Polleit sees it differently: "A proper diagnosis is necessary before you know the right remedy. Your government—and others—are dealing with the symptoms but not the causes." As any doctor will tell you, that is not in the patient's long-term interest.

United States and China Must Join Forces to Control Crisis

Michael Pettis

Michael Pettis is a finance professor at the Guanghua School of Management at Peking University and the author of The Volatility Machine: Emerging Economies and the Threat of Financial Collapse. *In the following viewpoint, Pettis states that no one should have been surprised by the global economic crisis because of the imbalances in liquidity and trade that started in the 1980s. He maintains that during this time, Americans started to consume more, China produced more, and banks in both countries offered more loans. This caused the bubble to burst in 2008. Pettis urges the United States and China to work together to help curb overspending in the United States and overproduction in China.*

As you read, consider the following questions:

1. According to Michael Pettis, what two reasons cause excess liquidity growth?

2. How much were Americans saving after 1998, according to the author?

3. According to the viewpoint, why did the People's Bank of China (PBC) have to create the yuan?

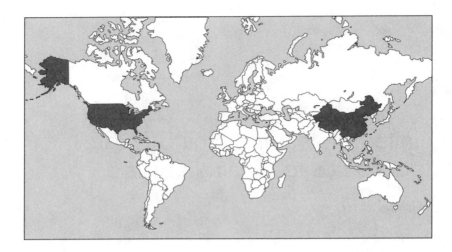

The two nations [United States and China] must coordinate fiscal and monetary policy to control the crisis they helped create, says Michael Pettis.

The surprising thing about the current financial crisis roiling the world is that there is surprise. While triggers for financial crises throughout history have been different, the underlying causes have been the same. Every financial crisis in history has been preceded by a long period of excess liquidity growth. It's no different this time, nor is the sharp debate now raging about finding the scapegoat. Without trying to apportion blame, it's clear though that the surge in US liquidity and the US-China trade imbalance that created this surge in liquidity have been major factors behind the current crisis, and policy makers in Washington and Beijing share the primary responsibility to readjust their economies.

Excess Liquidity Growth

Excess liquidity growth typically occurs for two reasons: First, financial innovation or new money sources can lead to sharp increases in underlying money, for example the development and expansion of joint stock banks in the 1820s, the securitisation of mortgages in the 1980s, or large gold or silver discoveries in the 19th century. Second, massive global imbalances are recycled like German reparations in the 1920s or petrodollars in the 1970s.

During the period of excess liquidity growth, several factors set the stage for the subsequent crisis: Asset prices rise as money flows into asset markets, risk appetite rises as risk premia decline and risky investments prove profitable, and the perceived value of liquidity declines as trading volume surges. When this happens, regulatory attempts to reduce risk in the financial system generally fail. When any part of the financial system is constrained from taking on risk, the market simply evades these constraints in one of three ways: It innovates around them, it generates or develops new and unregulated parts of the financial system, or it conceals regulatory violations.

The recent explosion of derivatives incorrectly blamed for the current crisis was simply an efficient way to accomplish all three, and was no more the real cause of the current crisis than investment trusts were in the 1920s or out-of-control real estate lending was in 1980s Japan. The financial system was simply adjusting, as it must and always does, to surging liquidity and rising risk appetite.

The recent liquidity surge, to which the current crisis is the inevitable denouement, had its roots in the 1980s, when the securitisation of US mortgages converted a huge pool of illiquid assets into highly liquid securities, and was subsequently reinforced by the recycling of the Japanese trade surplus with the US in mid-decade. The process took off, however, after 1998. During this time US household savings declined to rates never before seen and the US trade deficit, which until then had rarely exceeded 1 percent of GDP [gross domestic product], rose to levels never matched in US history.

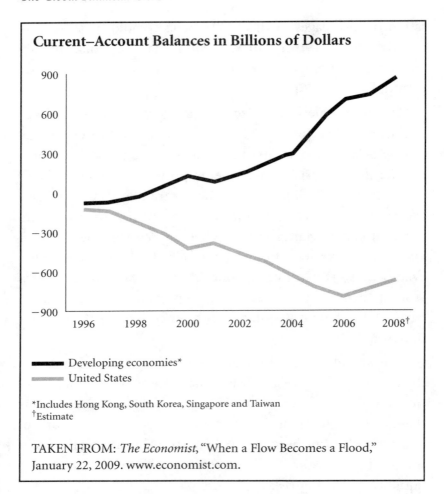

Current–Account Balances in Billions of Dollars

■■■■ Developing economies*
▬▬▬ United States

*Includes Hong Kong, South Korea, Singapore and Taiwan
†Estimate

TAKEN FROM: *The Economist*, "When a Flow Becomes a Flood," January 22, 2009. www.economist.com.

China Produces More than It Consumes

Also during this period several Asian countries, led by China, began running policies aimed at generating trade surpluses and accumulating foreign currency reserves, to the extent that net capital flows from developing countries soared to the highest recorded levels in history. It's notoriously difficult to sort out causality in balance-of-payments relationships, but the fact that this process seems to have begun in 1998 suggests that it may have been a reaction to the Asian crisis of 1997, a shocking event for Asian policy makers to this day.

The fundamental relationship in this global balance of payments was between China and the US. With Chinese policies aimed, explicitly or not, at promoting production and constraining consumption, China produced far more than it consumed.

As part of its trade surplus, China accumulated dollars, subsequently invested in the US. This capital export did not occur in the form of private investment, but rather as forced accumulation of foreign currency reserves, which were recycled back to the US largely in the form of purchases of US dollar assets by the People's Bank of China (PBC). Since China sets the value of its currency, the PBC had no choice but to accumulate reserves in this manner.

This recycling process functioned as a great liquidity generator for the world, converting US consumption into Chinese savings, which were recycled back into US financial markets through massive PBC purchases of US securities. There are several self-reinforcing aspects to this system that pushed it to the extremes it ultimately took. In the US the torrent of inward-bound liquidity boosted asset prices. As real estate and stocks surged, substantially raising US household wealth, households diverted a rising share of their income to consumption.

Americans Spend More, Save Less

At the same time since rising liquidity always forces financial institutions to adjust their balance sheets to accommodate money growth, they increased outstanding loans. With banks eager to lend, and households eager to fund consumption, it was only a question of time before household borrowing ballooned and an increasing share of current income was diverted to consumption rather than savings. In fact since the late 1940s US households have saved between 6 and 10 percent of US GDP, but after 1998 household savings began plummeting, to reach nearly zero by 2007—something which had never before happened.

Meanwhile in China, as foreign currency poured into the country via its trade surplus, the PBC had to create yuan to purchase the inflow. In China most new money creation ends up in banks, who primarily fund investment, as consumer lending is a negligible part of bank lending. The PBC tried to constrain excess credit growth, but it surged anyway, mostly off balance sheet, in rapid loan growth among policy banks, exempt from the loan constraints, or in the unregulated informal banking sector. As always, loose monetary policy resulted in explosive growth in financial risk-taking, even as regulators tried to constrain the growth.

With Chinese investment surging, industrial production grew faster than consumption and, concomitantly, real estate prices soared. As the gap between production and consumption grew, so did China's trade surplus, which resulted in more foreign currency pouring into the country, thus reinforcing the cycle.

Monetary Traps Cause Imbalance to Grow

This trade and capital relationship between the two countries, with each country locking itself unwillingly and accidentally into self-reinforcing monetary traps, caused the imbalances to get out of hand. It also ensured that adjustment would be brutal. With US asset markets now plunging and US banks unwilling to lend for consumption, one-half of the relationship is adjusting sharply. China's equally sharp and necessary adjustment should not have been a surprise.

We are now in the second stage of the crisis, in which trade-surplus countries must adjust after the forced adjustment in trade deficit countries. However, the US is so much larger than China, and it is adjusting so rapidly, there's a real risk that the Chinese economy will be overwhelmed. Policy makers, especially in the US and China, must ensure that this adjustment takes place in the least disruptive way possible.

This requires that as the major trade deficit and trade surplus countries, the US and China must coordinate fiscal and monetary policy so as to slow the process down.

US fiscal policies, in other words, should not be aimed at replacing collapsing US household demand with government demand. This would only perpetuate the imbalance. They should be aimed primarily at providing traction for Chinese fiscal policy, which ultimately must be responsible for creating enough demand to absorb Chinese overcapacity. Unfortunately it's far from obvious that policy makers, especially in China, understand the risk.

Periodical Bibliography

Alan S. Blinder "Six Errors on the Path to the Financial Crisis," *New York Times*, February 5, 2009.

Anand Chokkavelu "The Biggest Cause of the Financial Crisis," The Motley Fool, April 13, 2009. www.fool.com.

Steven Dunaway "Global Imbalances and the Financial Crisis," Council of Foreign Relations, March 2009. www.cfr.org.

James L. Gattuso "Meltdowns and Myths: Did Deregulation Cause the Financial Crisis?" Heritage Foundation, October 22, 2008. www.heritage.org.

Grinning Planet "'Casino Finance'—Snake Eyes for the Little Guy," January 4, 2009. www.grinning planet.com.

Home Buying Institute "Causes of Current U.S. Financial Crisis—And Why You Should Vote Democrat," October 5, 2008. www.homebuyinginstitute.com.

Paul Krugman "Reagan Did It," *New York Times*, May 31, 2009.

David Leonhardt "Bill Clinton, on His Economic Legacy," *New York Times*, May 27, 2009.

Richard A. Posner "A Failure of Capitalism: Reply to Alan Greenspan," The Daily Dish, May 24, 2009. http://andrewsullivan.theatlantic.com.

John B. Taylor "How Government Created the Financial Crisis," *Wall Street Journal*, February 9, 2009.

Greg Wood "Did Bush Cause the Financial Crisis?" *BBC News*, January 7, 2009. www.bbc.co.uk.

Thomas E. Woods Jr. "No, the Free Market Did Not Cause the Financial Crisis," LewRockwell.com, May 8, 2009. www.lewrockwell.com.

CHAPTER 2

Effects of the Global Financial Crisis on Wealthier Nations

In the United States, the Financial Crisis Creates Tent Cities and Homelessness

Kathy Sanborn

Kathy Sanborn is an author, journalist, and recording artist. In the following viewpoint, Sanborn argues that homelessness is growing in the United States thanks to the financial crisis. Sanborn notes reports from across the country that homelessness seems to be on the rise, resulting in strained shelters and tent cities. Sanborn suggests that 10 to 15 percent of the homeless are those who have lost their jobs because of the recession caused by the financial crisis.

As you read, consider the following questions:

1. According to Kathy Sanborn, who is to thank for the fact that Sacramento, California, is famous for its homeless tent city?

2. Was the estimate of 1,200 people in tent cities in Sacramento low or high, according to Sanborn?

3. According to Sanborn, why is the tent city in Seattle, Washington, called "Nickelsville"?

Homeless encampments around the country are mushrooming, much to the embarrassment of government officials, many of whom prefer to hear no evil, see no evil. In

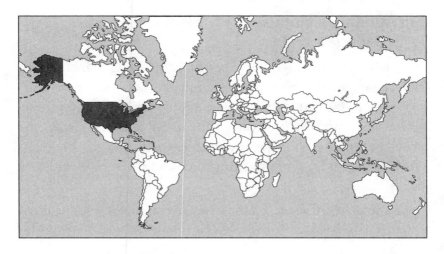

Fresno, California, a shantytown called "New Jack City" is host to newly poor, unemployed electricians and truck drivers, who share space with drug addicts and the mentally ill who have been homeless for years.

And, thanks to Oprah, Sacramento [California] is famous for its homeless tent city, featuring several hundred people residing in pitched tents bordering the American River. With refuse strewn everywhere, and no potable water or bathroom facilities, this celebrated shantytown is clearly a sanitation risk.

Almost as soon as the media ran with the story, plans were made to shut down the Sacramento tent city in the foreseeable future. City officials will relocate the homeless to other, presumably more sanitary, areas (e.g., at the site of the state fairgrounds, Cal Expo). According to the *Sacramento Bee*, "homeless campers" will be ousted in about four weeks, as the private property will be fenced off to ban the tent city population.

California's capital is not the only city to be brought to its knees by photos of disheveled citizens with nebulous futures. Reports of burgeoning tent cities in Nevada, Tennessee, and Washington State (just to name a few) have kept local governments hopping to fix the trouble before the media spotlight targets their own cities.

Sacramento's Homeless Problem Is Growing

Initial reports of huge numbers of people living in the tent city in Sacramento probably were inflated, we know now. Estimates of 1,200 tent dwellers were simply exaggerated by overzealous or slapdash journalists. Incorrect numbers aside, the problem remains: The new poor and the chronically homeless live side by side, with nothing but a cloth roof over their heads.

I spoke with Sister Libby, executive director of the now-infamous Loaves & Fishes in Sacramento, which provides charitable assistance to the hungry and homeless.

St. John's Shelter in Sacramento said they turn away 230 women and children each day, as opposed to the twenty turned away daily in 2007.

Sister Libby said,

"We have over two to three hundred folks here in the Sacramento tent city. At its height, about 2–3 new faces a day were showing up. Of the tent city population, 80–85% have been homeless for over a year. Only about 10–15% are the 'new poor'—those with a recent job loss or home foreclosure.

"We have seen a lot of new faces—mostly women with children—coming in to find shelter.

"Last year, according to Sacramento government statistics, the countywide homeless total was around 1,200 people. It's probably more like 1,400 now.

"Since they have decided to close the tent city in Sacramento and provide 150 extra shelter beds in other locations for these folks, I worry about the people who are mentally ill or have drug and alcohol issues—which comprise about 50% of the tent city residents. They aren't shelter-ready. What is the government going to do with them?"

Mayor Kevin Johnson said the city's shelter demand has increased "four-fold." The executive director of St. John's Shelter in Sacramento said they turn away 230 women and children each day, as opposed to the twenty turned away daily in 2007. These numbers indicate a dramatic explosion of growth in the homeless population, but many are hesitant to attribute this sudden rise in homelessness to the current economic downturn.

Other Cities Face Similar Problems

City officials in Fresno report three major homeless encampments adjacent to the downtown area, and smaller sites near the highways. All told, Fresno's homeless population is about two thousand people, living in shantytowns with grim names such as Taco Flats or the aforementioned New Jack City. Drugs, violence, and prostitution are common in the Fresno tent cities, as people react to the stress of living outdoors with no services—and no money.

Individuals in Seattle, Washington, who have lost their jobs and homes reside in tents in the back of a church parking lot, derogatorily called Nickelsville. Named for Seattle Mayor Greg Nickels, whom residents say doesn't much care about their plight, the Nickelsville shantytown is home to about one hundred campers a day.

Nashville, Tennessee, has its own problems with tent cities. According to NewsChannel5.com, Nashville has one large tent city south of the downtown area, with at least thirty additional homeless camps scattered throughout the region. There is a concern about this "huge surge in the number of encampments," and the issue has reached "urgent" proportions. Attributing the rise in homelessness to the faltering economy

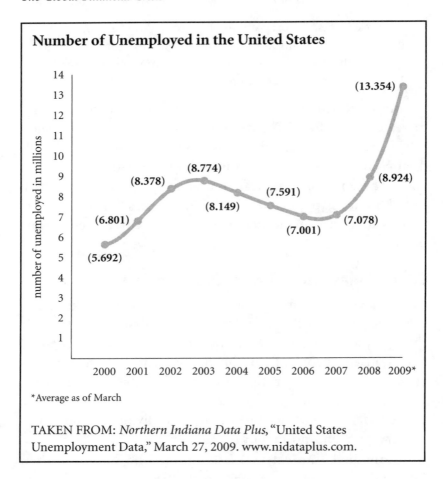

Number of Unemployed in the United States

number of unemployed in millions

(5.692)
(6.801)
(8.378)
(8.774)
(8.149)
(7.591)
(7.001)
(7.078)
(8.924)
(13.354)

2000 2001 2002 2003 2004 2005 2006 2007 2008 2009*

*Average as of March

TAKEN FROM: *Northern Indiana Data Plus*, "United States Unemployment Data," March 27, 2009. www.nidataplus.com.

that brings with it increased foreclosures and job layoffs, city officials are seeking answers—and fast—to their local homeless crisis.

At least 10–15% of homeless individuals are the "new poor," or those who have recently lost their jobs and homes.

In Reno, Nevada, officials closed a tent city in 2008 that housed about 160 residents. Now, the sidewalks of Reno serve as beds to some sixty homeless people with nowhere else to go. There are homeless camps on Record Street, and local merchants believe their business is down because of the sea of homeless vagabonds invading store sidewalks and blocking customer access to shops.

Reno officials are attempting to prevent another tent city from emerging in the summer of 2009, but with less revenue available for alternative housing, this remains to be seen.

What can we conclude from the rapid increase in homelessness across the nation? The facts are clear: there are more people, especially women and children, who are out on the streets, without a dime. At least 10–15% of homeless individuals are the "new poor," or those who have recently lost their jobs and homes. We can be certain that if the economy doesn't improve soon, there will be more of the new poor pitching their tents in shantytowns across America—maybe in your neighborhood.

Canada Will Not Suffer a Subprime Mortgage Crisis

Jonathan Kay

Jonathan Kay is a writer for Canada's National Post *and has also written for* Harper's, *the* New York Times, *and other publications. In the following viewpoint, Kay argues that Canada will not suffer a financial meltdown such as the one in the United States. Kay notes that, unlike America, Canadians did not build up high levels of debt and did not experience a housing bubble. In addition, Kay argues, Canadian banks did not make nearly as many bad mortgage loans and did not repackage and sell loans through complicated financial instruments. As a result, Canada is financially in a much better position than the United States.*

As you read, consider the following questions:

1. According to Jonathan Kay, is it common in Canada for homeowners to owe banks more than their homes are worth?

2. On average, at the time of the article, how did Canadian home prices compare to what they were in 1989, as the author reports?

3. At the time of the article, was the percentage of Canadian homes in 90-day arrears higher or lower than it had been six years previously?

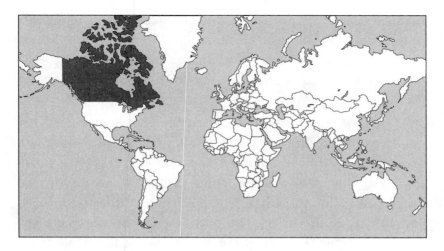

I know very little about the world financial markets, or even about basic financial concepts. When *Financial Post* types talk about EBITDA [a measure of a company's cash flow], I assume they're talking about the baby soybeans they serve you in Japanese restaurants. And yet, I was still able to understand this very reassuring Sept. 25 [2008] report from Scotiabank that explains, quite persuasively, why Canada isn't going to suffer the same sort of subprime-mortgage-fueled financial market meltdown that's wreaked so much havoc in the United States.

Canada Has Less Debt and Better Regulations

To make a simple report even simpler, here are the main points:

Less debt. In Canada, household liabilities as a percentage of assets sits at 20%—close to the stable, sustainable level it's been at since the late 1980s. In the United States, the figure sits at 26%, after spiking radically upward over the last decade.

Less crappy mortgages. Canada's subprime mortgage market (to the extent the bottom end of our mortgage market can even be called "subprime" in the American sense) represents only about one in every 20 mortgages. In the United States, the peak figure was about one in *six*. Astoundingly, up to a quarter of mortgages issued in the 2004–2006 period were in the subprime category.

Less debt, Part 2. In the United States, homeowners' net equity as a percentage of home value has plummeted from around 65% to 45% over the last two decades, with more than half that drop coming since 2000. In Canada, on the other hand, this ratio has remained stable at between 65% and 70% since the 1980s. The phenomenon of mortgages going "underwater"—with homeowners owing the bank more than their homes are worth—is now tragically common in the United States. In Canada, it is virtually unknown.

Canada's subprime mortgage market represents only about one in every 20 mortgages. In the United States, the peak figure was about one in six.

Less off-balance-sheet mortgages. The frenzy of mortgage securitization [pooling and repackaging] that gripped the United States in recent years never really took off here. According to Scotiabank, "The majority of mortgages are held on balance sheet in Canada, with only 24% having been securitized." That's huge, because it is the radioactive quality of these securities—many of which contain a tangled welter of mortgages of varying quality—that has really sunk the U.S. credit market: Since no one knows how much these complex instruments are really worth, they still haven't established an equilibrium price level, thereby freezing the credit market for any entity that has a large number of them on their books. (What's more, even those 24% have mostly been securitized through the CMHC [Canada Mortgage and Housing Corporation], a Crown corp. with government backing.)

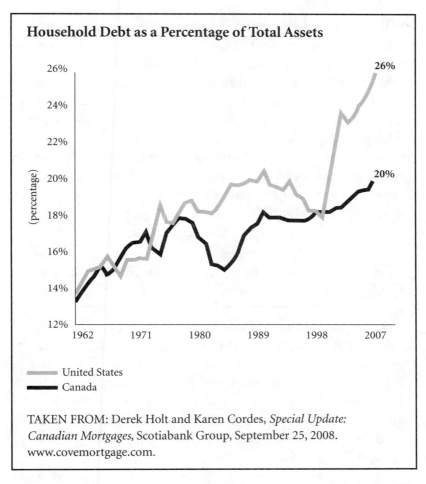

Household Debt as a Percentage of Total Assets

TAKEN FROM: Derek Holt and Karen Cordes, *Special Update: Canadian Mortgages*, Scotiabank Group, September 25, 2008. www.covemortgage.com.

Smarter bankers, smarter standards. Finally, there is the fact that Canada simply has a different—and more prudent—banking culture: "Unlike many U.S. banks, Canada banks continue to apply prudent underwriting standards. In other words, they have always checked, and continue to check, incomes, verify job status, asks for sales contracts, etc., such that all those questions your banker asks in Canada have a purpose that somehow got lost on many American bankers. The no-income-no-job-no-asset ('Ninja') style, here-are-the-keys-to-your-brand-new-home lending just didn't take hold in Canada."

Canada Had No Bubble

Looking beyond the Scotiabank report, I can see some other factors that should provide Canadians with comfort:

No bubble in the housing market. On average, Canadian home prices are roughly 200% what they were in 1989. In the United States, the corresponding ratio peaked at 260% before crashing down to 220%. In Canada, the more typical experience is that of my home, Toronto, which has witnessed steady increases in the 4–5% range every year, but none of the sudden surges and troughs that whipsawed home buyers in U.S. markets such as Miami have witnessed.

A prudent, risk-averse, well-regulated Canadian real estate and mortgage community . . . has avoided the pitfalls swallowing up the United States.

Fewer foreclosure notices—a lot fewer. This is the most shocking stat of all. In the United States, a full 4.5% of mortgages are in 90-day arrears (i.e., the local sheriff is ready to move in and tack a notice to the door). In Canada, the figure is *one 20th* that level—just 0.27%. Amazingly, while the U.S. figure of 4.5% represents a doubling of the 2002 level of 2.2%, Canada's 0.27% level reflects a halving from the (still low) level of 0.5% six years ago.

All in all, what do these figures show? A prudent, risk-averse, well-regulated Canadian real estate and mortgage community that—on both the seller, mortgager and buyer sides—has avoided the pitfalls swallowing up the United States. It's something that Canadians might want to remember the next time Stéphane Dion or one of the other opposition party leaders starts sputtering fatuously about Stephen Harper's "Bush-style" economic policies.

Australia's Economy Remains Bound Up with That of the United States

Sean Carmody

Sean Carmody lives in Sydney, Australia, and works in the financial markets. In the following viewpoint, he notes that before the crisis many people argued that Australia's economy was no longer linked to that of Western nations. Carmody says that Australia, however, like the United States, had high levels of debt and inflated (though not as severely inflated) home prices. Moreover, Australian financial institutions were heavily invested in the U.S. financial system and were hit hard by the banking crisis. Australia, Carmody argues, has not escaped the global downturn, and its economy remains linked to that of the West.

As you read, consider the following questions:

1. According to many commentators, do any significant risks remain for housing prices in Australia?

2. What was Australia's net foreign debt in 2007, as the author reports?

3. At the time Sean Carmody wrote this viewpoint, had Australian banks required cash infusions from the government?

Sean Carmody, "Australia and the Global Financial Crisis," A Stubborn Mule's Perspective, October 25, 2008. Reproduced by permission. http://www.stubbornmule.net/2008/10/australia-and-the-gfc.

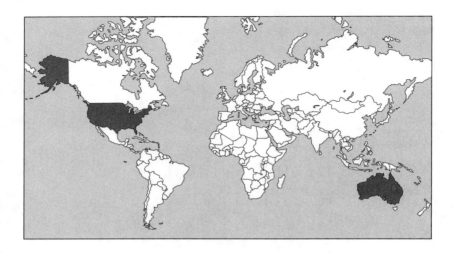

A year ago [2007], many commentators were extolling the idea that Australia's economy had "de-coupled" from the United States and Europe, and would continue to be powered by the rapid growth of China and other developing nations. Concerns about inflation meant that interest rates were rising and many felt Australia would escape the incipient economic slowdown in the developing world. Events have instead unfolded differently. The federal government has taken the extraordinary step of guaranteeing deposits held in all Australian banks, building societies and credit unions and the Reserve Bank of Australia has delivered an unexpected 1% cut in interest rates, citing heightened instability in financial markets and deteriorating prospects for global growth. This was an extraordinary turnaround. It is, of course, the result of Australia becoming ensnared in the global financial crisis that began in mid-2007 and has intensified ever since. But how and why did Australia get caught up in a mess that started with falling property prices in the US?

The Australian Crisis Mirrored America's

The crisis has unfolded in stages. First came the bursting of the housing bubble in the United States. This in turn led to a cycle in which the prices of many mortgage-backed securities plunged, triggering the liquidation of a number of hedge funds [investment funds permitted by regulators to undertake more activities than are usual for other kinds of funds] holding these securities, which in turn led to further collapses in security prices. Following this hedge fund liquidation phase, the focus of concern moved to banks. Banks were slow to admit to the extent of their exposure to mortgage-backed securities and related derivatives, which led to a breakdown of trust in the markets. Banks became extremely reluctant to lend to one another and, despite repeated efforts by central banks to inject large amounts of cash into the banking system, the result was a liquidity crisis. This phase of the crisis has been both longer and more severe than most observers expected and has resulted in sweeping changes to the US banking landscape through both mergers and collapses. While the United States has been at the epicentre, each phase of the crisis has been echoed in Australia.

Property prices rose at a similar rate to the United States and ever since 2002–03 the Australian household savings rate has been negative.

Back in June 2005, the *Economist* published these prophetic words: "Never before have real house prices risen so fast, for so long, in so many countries. Property markets have been frothing from America, Britain and Australia to France, Spain and China. Rising property prices helped to prop up the world economy after the stock-market bubble burst in 2000. What if the housing boom now turns to bust?" These frothy property prices were fuelled by a combination of low interest rates, loosening lending standards, growing consumer appetite for debt and extensive use of securitisation [pooling and repackaging], which effectively allowed home buyers to access capital from all around the world.

It has been estimated that from 2004 to 2006, more than 20% of new US mortgages were taken out by "subprime" borrowers with poor credit histories and limited capacity to service their loans. These borrowers instead relied on ever rising property prices allowing them to sell for a profit or refinance their mortgages at a lower rate once they had accumulated more equity. Of course, once prices started to fall, these borrowers began to fall behind in their payments or simply to walk away from a debt now much larger than the diminished value of their home.

In some ways, things were not very different in Australia. Property prices rose at a similar rate to the United States and ever since 2002–03 the Australian household savings rate has been negative. Until very recently, borrowers also faced repeated interest rate rises on their growing debt. However, Australia's subprime market was much smaller than the United States at only about 2% of mortgages and while the United States still has significant excess housing supply, Australia still faces a shortage of housing. As a result, despite rising delinquency rates, Australia has as yet escaped a vicious bursting of the housing bubble. Nevertheless, many commentators argue that significant risks remain for property prices in Australia.

The US Banking Crisis Hurt Australia

When it came to the second phase of the crisis, Australia was not so lucky. Many investors held securities with direct exposure to the ailing US subprime mortgage-backed market. Two prominent casualties were high-yield funds managed by Basis Capital and Absolute Capital. Mortgage-backed securities that had been repackaged in the form of collateralized debt obligations (CDOs) had also been widely distributed to so-called middle market investors: local councils, universities, schools and hospitals. Non-bank mortgage lender RAMS also found itself in trouble. RAMS was heavily reliant on short-term funding, much of which it sourced from US investors who

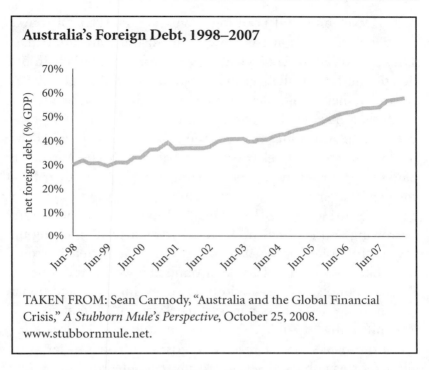

Australia's Foreign Debt, 1998–2007

TAKEN FROM: Sean Carmody, "Australia and the Global Financial Crisis," *A Stubborn Mule's Perspective*, October 25, 2008. www.stubbornmule.net.

were no longer interested in purchasing asset-backed commercial paper [a security sold to meet short-term debt obligations] regardless of whether the underlying mortgages were in the United States or elsewhere. Unable to fund itself, RAMS became the first Australian corporate victim to the financial crisis. Other non-bank mortgage lenders also came under pressure as global securitization markets effectively shut down. The one bright spot was that, unlike European and US banks, Australian banks appeared to have minimal direct exposure to subprime mortgage-backed securities and their derivatives [financial contracts whose value is based on something else such as mortgages] on their balance sheets.

As the crisis shifted into the liquidity [or credit] phase, the impact on Australia intensified. Institutions that were heavily reliant on financing, particularly from offshore, found it more and more expensive to refinance maturing debts. Among the companies caught in the crunch were Centro, MFS [Limited],

ABC [Developmental] Learning [Centres] and Allco. Of course the biggest institutional borrowers in Australia are the banks. They had come to rely increasingly on offshore markets in order to fund Australia's growing borrowing habits. By 2007, Australia's net foreign debt exceeded $500 billion, representing more than 50% of the country's annual gross domestic product [GDP]. A significant proportion of this debt is raised by banks. Despite their relatively clean balance sheets, Australian banks were forced to pay the same high margins on their borrowings that investors were demanding of European and US banks. Even money markets [financial markets for short-term borrowing and lending] in Australia were affected, pushing up the interest rates banks had to pay for short-dated borrowings. Like other central banks around the world, the Reserve Bank responded to the liquidity crisis by injecting additional cash into the system. As part of this effort, in September 2007 it significantly expanded the range of collateral it would accept from banks in exchange for funds, even going so far as to allow mortgage-backed securities, albeit highly rated ones. Despite the global and local turmoil, the Reserve Bank remained concerned about inflation, raising rates four times during the credit crisis. In an effort to recoup some of their soaring funding costs, banks broke with tradition and raised mortgage rates over and above the Reserve Bank moves. . . .

With tighter lending standards, weak consumer and business confidence, and signs of slowing international demand for Australian commodities, Australia is unlikely to escape this phase of the financial crisis.

Australia's Real Economy Has Not Escaped

Despite the funding challenges faced by the banks and the volatility in Australian fixed income and equity markets, it was not until September 2008 that alarm spread outside financial markets. As governments around the world began guaranteeing bank depositors, Australians began to realise that their own deposits were not guaranteed. This led to fears that Australian financial institutions, particularly regional banks and credit unions, could experience a run by depositors, something that none could withstand regardless of the underlying strength of their balance sheets. Fearing the catastrophic effect this could have on the Australian economy, the federal government swiftly moved from plans to guarantee sums of up to $20,000 to announcing on 12 October 2008 a comprehensive guarantee of all retail deposits for three years. At the same time, they announced a guarantee scheme for bank wholesale borrowing to ensure Australian banks could compete for funding against other government-guaranteed banks around the world. Nevertheless, Australian banks still have had no need of the capital injections received by many banks around the world.

While moves by governments and regulators around the world appear to have averted systemic financial failure, concerns remain about the impact the global financial crisis will have on the real economy. With tighter lending standards, weak consumer and business confidence, and signs of slowing international demand for Australian commodities, Australia is unlikely to escape this phase of the financial crisis. The government hopes that a $10.4 billion stimulus package will help protect Australia from the anticipated global recession, but few commentators still believe that Australia's economy has "de-coupled" from the United States and the rest of the developed world. Mind you, that is partly because Asia and developing nations around the world now seem well and truly coupled to the US-led financial crisis.

The European Union Is Buckling Under the Crisis

Edward Hugh

Edward Hugh is a Barcelona-based macroeconomist. In the following viewpoint, he argues that the financial crisis has hurt nations throughout Europe. He states that Germany has been hard hit, and that it is in no position to act as a savior. Instead, Hugh says, the European Union (EU) needs to issue EU bonds and start to print money in order to prevent deflation and contraction. Europe, Hugh claims, has been in denial about the extent of the crisis and must act swiftly if the European Union is to survive.

As you read, consider the following questions:

1. According to Edward Hugh, what might Spanish unemployment rise to in 2010?
2. Which two Eastern European nations face the current worst-case economic scenarios in Europe, according to Hugh?
3. According to Hugh, in the current economic situation, for what is "quantitative easing" a euphemism?

As [Russian novelist] Leo Tolstoy might put it, all of Europe's economies are feeling pretty unhappy right now, but each is unhappy in its own unique way. Nowhere have the

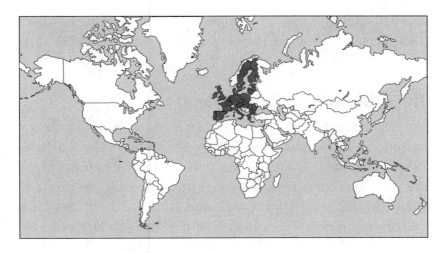

effects of the crisis been felt more acutely than in the "peripheral" countries on Europe's southern, northwestern and eastern edges. As the recession worsens, these countries are looking toward Europe's traditional center in hopes of salvation, seemingly unaware that the center itself is struggling to hold, as countries such as Germany and Austria battle with their own version of the meltdown.

The feeling is growing that Europe's problems are not local or national ones, but that it is the eurozone itself . . . that is fundamentally flawed.

As a consequence, the feeling is growing that Europe's problems are not local or national ones, but that it is the eurozone itself [including those nations that have adopted the euro currency]—in its conception and its architecture—that is fundamentally flawed, lacking the ability to come to the aid of individual countries in difficulty. Some analysts even worry that we might be witnessing the beginning of the end of the European experiment altogether.

The good news is that Europe can be saved. Rescuing Europe's problem economies will take much more than a simple bailout, though. It is going to require nothing less than a complete recasting of the continent's entire political and financial architecture.

The Crisis in Spain and Ireland

We begin our tour in Spain and Ireland, both until recently considered outstanding pupils by the European Central Bank (ECB) and major economic success stories. The two countries are now in serious trouble as they struggle with the unwinding of a property boom that has its roots in the ECB's ultra expansive monetary policy. Spain, Europe's fifth-largest economy, entered its first recession in 15 years at the end of last year [2008] and is now suffering from 15 percent unemployment, a figure that might rise to 20 percent or more by 2010. Forecasts for Spanish GDP [gross domestic product] growth in 2009 range from minus 3 percent to minus 5 percent, but the contraction could easily extend into 2010, 2011, and beyond. The Spanish government is still essentially in denial about the scale of the correction needed and has been busy trying to spend its way out of trouble, with the predictable negative consequence that the country's once solid fiscal surplus is now spiraling downward into deficit at breathtaking speed. Indeed, the European Commission (EC) has already initiated an excess deficit procedure against Spain.

As for Ireland, it was not so long ago that the country's economy was experiencing a boom of such proportions that it came to be known as the "Celtic Tiger." Now, the tiger is tanking. The EC forecasts a 5 percent contraction in GDP this year; unemployment is widely expected to hit 11 percent; and house prices have plummeted. As a result, the Irish fiscal deficit is expected to rise to 9.4 percent in 2009. Again, the EC has opened an excess deficit procedure, and the country is being threatened with losing its AAA debt rating [its debt will be considered less safe, or less likely to be repaid].

The Crisis in Eastern Europe and Scandinavia

The EU's [European Union's] most recent members are also feeling the chilly winds of recession. If anything, Eastern European economies and credit ratings are even less capable than their Western counterparts of weathering dramatic increases in debt levels. Thus, in the case of those countries having a significant home-banking presence, such as Latvia and Hungary, the support of external organizations—the EU, the World Bank, the International Monetary Fund (IMF)— becomes rapidly necessary when their banks start having liquidity problems [problems finding cash to pay debts]. Then, as a direct result of the consequent bailouts, the countries' debt-to-GDP ratios start to rise, putting their eurozone membership in jeopardy. If something isn't done soon, these two countries, and possibly others, are headed for a self-perpetuating process of indebtedness with only one end point: sovereign default.

Latvia and Hungary may be the current worst-case scenarios, but the list of walking wounded is growing by the day. Romania and Bulgaria are now in "informal consultations" with the IMF, while Slovakia and Slovenia (the two Eastern European countries that actually made it into the eurozone) hurtle off into deep recessions. What's more, the chilly wind has now spread even further north, beyond the Baltics and into Scandinavia. Sweden is in the middle of a much more serious recession than previously thought. Official figures for the fourth quarter of last year reveal that GDP contracted 2.4 percent quarter-on-quarter in the final three months of last year, equivalent to an annualized decline of 9.3 percent. Denmark is in the middle of a housing bust, and its economy has contracted as households spend less and the global financial crisis saps demand for the country's exports. Finnish output also slumped, by 1.3 percent, the most in 17 years, in the fourth quarter of 2008. Certainly the situation is less severe in the north, but in addition to the homegrown recession, Sweden's troubled banking sector now labors under the growing weight of debt defaults in the Baltics and other parts of Europe.

It is by now abundantly clear that many of Europe's leaders simply haven't yet grasped the severity of the problems the continent faces.

The European Center Is Ill-Equipped to Help

With the periphery on the ropes, all eyes have been turning to the center for help, particularly to Germany. Peer Steinbrück, Germany's finance minister, has had to face the cameras on an almost daily basis to answer a barrage of press questions about how equipped the EU is to handle all the looming bailouts, as if reaching for the German checkbook were the magic remedy to cure all ills.

Unfortunately, nothing could be further from the truth. Germany has itself been bruised and battered, first in the U.S. subprime turmoil, then in Ireland, and now in Eastern Europe. Its export-driven economy has suffered the impact of recession after recession among its main customers. The economic slump in the final quarter of 2008 proved worse than feared, with the country posting the sharpest fall in GDP since it was reunified in the early 1990s. And there is evidently worse to come, because the German private sector shrank in February at its fastest rate in more than a decade. Many economists now anticipate a contraction of about 5 percent for 2009.

The *Financial Times* correspondent Wolfgang Munchau has been complaining bitterly of late—and with good reason—about the extraordinary narrow-mindedness of Europe's economic and political leadership in the face of the current crisis. But more than narrow-mindedness, what Europeans face is innocence and an inability to react, which frankly, might be worse. I say "innocence" because it is by now abundantly clear that many of Europe's leaders simply haven't yet grasped the severity of the problems the continent faces (especially in Spain, or even Germany, let alone in Eastern Europe), and I say "inability to react," because Europe has always and forever been moving too little and too late. The initial response to the banking crisis last October provides just one clear example about how it is one thing to make promises to guarantee the banking sector, and quite another thing to live up to them.

Ten years of bad craftsmanship cannot be put straight in a day, but Europe is going to have to try. The EU now badly needs to remedy its institutional deficiencies to address its crisis overload problem. Fortunately, remedies are available, even if getting Europe's leaders to talk about them is akin to leading a reluctant father-to-be up to the altar.

Issue Bonds and Print Money

First, EU (rather than exclusively national) bonds can be created. These will effectively give Europe a fiscal capacity that is, for all intents and purposes, equivalent to that of the U.S. Treasury. Second, given the deflation problem, the European Central Bank can now follow the Bank of England and the Swiss National Bank by entering the next tier of quantitative easing, expanding its balance sheet and starting to buy those crisp new EU bonds in the primary market.

(Quantitative easing, which is simply a generic way of referring to all the recent attempts to boost money supply when interest rates fall close to zero, becomes in this particular case a euphemism for "printing money," with the unusual characteristic that this time, inflation is exactly what we are looking for. And if we don't get it, well, as Paul Krugman wrote in a

Eastern Europe Is Going Backward

The view in the East is that the onset of the world economic crisis has suddenly reversed globalization. Hundreds of thousands of Poles, Bulgarians and Romanians had found relatively well-paid jobs in Western EU countries, but now an army of migrant workers is making its way back home to the East. At the same time, the capital the region so desperately needs is flowing in the other direction, as Western banks and investors pull out their money.

The fact that the crisis in the West is now pulling down the East is largely attributable to a single mistake. For years, Eastern Europeans took out loans denominated in euros, Swiss francs and Scandinavian kroner. The loans stimulated domestic consumption and allowed the economies to grow. Many new member states imported more goods than they exported. Now the mountains of debt are high. . . .

Citizens in the new EU [European Union] member states can expect to see their wages stagnate at lower levels compared with those in the West, assuming they have not already been cut drastically. In addition to mass layoffs, ailing Eastern European business owners have resorted to wage cuts of up to 30 percent in recent months. And someone who is out of work in the East quickly finds him- or herself in a very tight spot. Governments are out of money, and social services were cut back in many places during the boom years.

Jan Puhl, "Eastern Europe's Economic Crash,"
Spiegel Online, March 23, 2009. www.spiegel.de.

recent the *New York Times* op-ed on Spain, we run the risk of ending up with a European economy that is depressed and tending toward deflation for years to come.)

Third, the rules of the Maastricht Treaty [1992 treaty that created the eurozone] should be rewritten to give the eurozone rapid access to the highly vulnerable countries of Eastern Europe. These countries have been suffering, either directly (in the case of countries whose currencies are pegged to the euro—the Baltics and Bulgaria) or indirectly (in the case of countries with floating currencies, but whose economies are tied through exports to Western Europe—Poland, the Czech Republic, Hungary, and Romania) from the gravitational pull of the currency union. They need short-term protection, followed by long-term nurturing, and the eurozone structure is itself the best incubator we have at hand.

What Europe badly needs to do at this point is restore confidence—confidence that it is not in denial . . . that it has the instruments at its disposal to resolve the problem, and that it is up to the task of implementing them.

The Crisis Can Be an Opportunity

The most important thing to realize is that the arrival of deflation [falling prices] is not only a threat; it is also an opportunity. Having the power (nay the necessity) to print money should give Europe's central administration one hell of clout should it need to use it, and it will. As Joaquín Almunia, EU commissioner for economic and monetary affairs, said earlier this month, "You would have to be crazy to want to leave the eurozone right now," given the economic climate. It's precisely this fear that should serve as a persuasive stick to accompany that attractive financial carrot. (Assuming Europe's leaders understand that, in this case at least, sparing the rod would only amount to spoiling not only the child, but all the brothers and sisters and aunts and uncles, too.)

So though the first argument in favor of EU bonds might be an entirely pragmatic one—that it doesn't make sense for subsidiary components of EU, Inc., to pay more to borrow money when the credit guarantee of the parent entity can get it for them far cheaper—the longer-term argument is that the ability to issue such bonds might well enable the EC to become something it has long dreamed of becoming: an internal credit rating agency for EU national debt.

What Europe badly needs to do at this point is restore confidence—confidence that it is not in denial about the underlying severity of the economic problem, that it has the instruments at its disposal to resolve the problem, and that it is up to the task of implementing them. This restoration of confidence that "we have the means, we have the will, and we are going to finish the job" is what, more than anything else, is lacking right now. Otherwise, Europe will be back to local, national, piecemeal solutions; to hoping in vain for a German savior (when Germany itself is struggling); and to rising bond spreads and growing economic chaos. As World Bank President Robert Zoellick told the *Financial Times* recently, "It's 20 years after Europe was united in 1989—what a tragedy if you allow Europe to split again."

In Iceland, an Economic Miracle Ended in Disaster

Andrew Pierce

Andrew Pierce is an assistant editor at the Daily Telegraph. *In the following viewpoint, he reports that Iceland was a small, relatively poor country until recently, when its economy and standard of living expanded rapidly. This expansion was linked to the rapid growth of the banking sector, which began in the mid-1990s. When the global financial crisis crippled banking, however, Iceland faced a major crisis. Now, according to Pierce, the massive gains of the last few years may all disappear.*

As you read, consider the following questions:

1. What is the life expectancy the author cites for men in Iceland?

2. According to Andrew Pierce, young businessmen in Iceland did not want their country to depend on what for its principal source of wealth?

3. Over a five-year period during the boom, by how much did the average Icelandic family's wealth grow, according to Pierce?

Iceland had ousted Norway from the head of the UN's league table of 177 countries that compared per-capita income, education, health care and life expectancy—which, at 80.55 years for males, was third highest in the world.

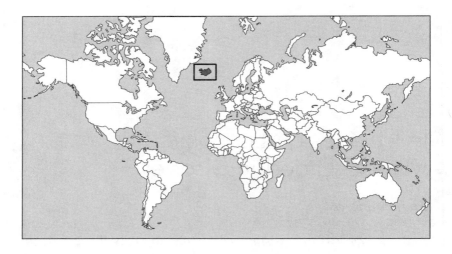

This was only one in a string of glowing assessments of a country (population 313,000) which had pulled off a modern-day economic miracle. No wonder they are also said to be the happiest people on the planet. The inhabitants of this newly discovered Utopia, with its much-admired free health and education systems, bought the most books, owned most mobile telephones per head, and included the highest proportion of working women in the world.

Iceland overreached itself in spectacular fashion, and the party is coming to a messy end.

Iceland had also presided over the fastest expansion of a banking system anywhere in the world. Little did anyone know that the expansion once so admired would go on to saddle the country with liabilities in excess of $100 billion—liabilities that now dwarf its gross domestic product of $14 billion.

Iceland overreached itself in spectacular fashion, and the party is coming to a messy end.

Yesterday, trading in the shares of six major financial institutions was suspended as the government sought to avert meltdown.

Sigurdur Einarsson, chairman, Kaupthing Bank, warned against people being too alarmist.

> Over the years we have built a strong and well-diversified bank. We have some of the strongest capital ratios in the European bank sector. We've got good asset quality and a highly diversified loan portfolio.
>
> Kaupthing has and continues to manage its business prudently and, with our strong fundamentals, we are naturally concerned when we hear malicious rumours and sensationalism about Kaupthing being reflected irresponsibly. We ask people to look at the facts, not rumour and inuendo.

Meanwhile, Icelandic interest rates have been catapulted to 15.5 percent, peaks not seen in Britain since Black Wednesday, in an attempt to rein in inflation. The krona's freefall on the international currency markets is surpassed only by the catastrophic failure of Zimbabwean currency.

One of the country's three banks, Glitnir, has been nationalised; another wants money from its customers. Foreign currency is running out as international banks refuse pleas to lend money.

No longer smiling, office workers hurry home wondering out loud if they will have jobs to go to by the end of the week. Car showrooms are deserted. Estate agents are closing early. There are few takers for the thousands of unsold houses on their books. An unexpected cold spell is keeping many people inside their homes, another reason why the shops, many of which have discount sales, are quiet.

The speed with which Iceland rose and then fell to earth has bewildered not just the islanders but also Geir Haarde, the Prime Minister who has spent the past four days locked away with his advisers in Reykjavik. He emerged on Monday to announce new powers for the country's financial regulator:

"We were faced with the real possibility that the national economy would be sucked into the global banking swell and end in national bankruptcy. The legislation is necessary to avoid that fate."

The dramatic change in Iceland, from the poor relation of Europe to one of its wealthiest and apparently most successful, and now back again, dates from the mid-1990s with the privatisation of the banks and the founding of the country's Stock Exchange.

The free market reforms unleashed a new generation of thrusting, young businessmen, many of whom picked up their banking trade in the United States. They were determined that their country would no longer have to rely on fishing for its principal source of wealth; they loathed the international perception of Iceland as a parochial nation of farmers and fishermen who could not hold their own on the world business stage.

The dramatic change in Iceland, from the poor relation of Europe to one of its wealthiest . . . and now back again, dates from the mid-1990s with the privatisation of the banks and the founding of the country's Stock Exchange.

They had learnt at school all about the last Cod War with Britain, in 1976, when Iceland unilaterally extended its territorial waters, desperate to increase the financial yield from its trawler fleet. So, in keeping with the traditions of their Viking ancestors, the new army of corporate raiders went overseas to seek their fortune.

Kaupthing, one of the three banks at centre of the debt crisis, is not even in the top 100 of the world's biggest banks. But its influence on the British economy is out of all proportion to its 124th ranking. In five years it has underwritten more than £3 billion in debt to help finance British deals.

Instability and Violence in Iceland

The tiny, North Atlantic island of Iceland, whose economy already lies in tatters, was plunged into further crisis on Monday [January 26, 2009] as the coalition government collapsed amid violent protests on the streets. . . .

Mr. Haarde [prime minister of Iceland] had called for early elections just last week, saying he would not lead his Independence Party into the new elections because he needed treatment for throat cancer. However, he was forced to disband the government yesterday. . . .

In recent days the daily protests have become more violent. The police were forced to use tear gas last week for the first time since 1949. Following the violent clashes, Mr. Haarde had called for early elections, but his plan, along with the economy, now lies in ruins.

Ciaran Walsh,
"Icelandic Government Falls—
Will Europe Learn from Haarde Lesson?"
RT Online, *January 27, 2009. www.russiatoday.ru.*

This is why the bankruptcy is not only adding to the turmoil on London Stock Exchange—which at one point lost eight percent of its value—but also sending ripples through the British High Street. Baugur, the Icelandic investment house, has amassed large stakes in retailers including Hamleys, House of Fraser, Oasis, Debenhams and Iceland the frozen food store. Question marks hang over their future.

Kaupthing lent the money to Baugur to finance its investment in Arcadia back in 2001, which it then sold on to the British billionaire Philip Green. It also snapped up the UK merchant bank Singer & Friedlander for £547 million in 2005—a company which has helped bankroll some of Britain's best known entrepreneurs, such as Gordon Ramsay. It also advised the sportswear tycoon Mike Ashley on his troubled £134 million purchase of Newcastle United football club. Kaupthing was also a big investor in the London property market, which has become another millstone round the bank's neck.

The Icelandic bankers were able to raise billions for their expansion from the booming new Stock Market in Reykjavik and because of Iceland's extraordinary well-funded pension system.

For decades one of the poorest countries in Europe, Iceland could finally celebrate as the average family's wealth grew by 45 percent in five years. GDP accelerated at between four to six percent a year and the wealth was invested in property that, in turn, fuelled an unsustainable boom in house prices. In the good times, credit companies sprang up offering 100 percent loans, many in foreign currency such as Japanese yen or Swiss francs. But with the krona in freefall, some loans have doubled in size and thousands are defaulting.

Some did counsel caution. In 2004, Björn Gudmundsson, an economist with Landsbanki, said: "We think the economy will cool rapidly in 2007. Much of the investment in infrastructure will come to an end then." But the dealmakers thought the good times would last forever. In the same year that Gudmundsson sounded his warning, Icelandic investors spent £895 million on shares in British companies alone.

It was almost inevitable that when the international credit crisis unleashed the worst financial tsunami the world had seen since 1929, there was little that Iceland, which disbanded its armed forces 700 years ago, could do to repel the shock waves. Iceland has guaranteed all its savers deposits, but could not extend this guarantee to the hundreds of thousands of British savers who have invested money in their Internet savings banks.

The mood of crisis was heightened further when the Government suspended all public service broadcasting, a measure usually reserved for volcano warnings. The chairman of the opposition left-green party, Steingrímur Sigfússon, has called for a coalition government to lead Iceland through its financial emergency.

The trade unions, meanwhile, are pressing for Iceland to begin talks about becoming part of the European Union, which the government has been reluctant to join for years. The pension funds have now also agreed to help the Government by selling assets.

The mood of crisis was heightened further when the Government suspended all public service broadcasting, a measure usually reserved for volcano warnings.

It took a while, though, for the penny to drop. As recently as this spring, when questions were being asked about the economy, the country was in denial.

Dagur Eggertsson, a former mayor of Reykjavik, said: "Someone called it 'bumblebee economics' because it is hard to figure out how it flies, but it does, and very nicely, too." The bumblebee, though, like the billionaires who thought they could buy up the British high street, is no longer flying high.

The Crisis Fuels Unrest in France, Britain, China, and Russia

Thomas Hüetlin, Andreas Lorenz, Christian Neef, Matthias Schepp, and Stefan Simons

Thomas Hüetlin, Andreas Lorenz, Christian Neef, Matthias Schepp, and Stefan Simons are staff writers at Der Spiegel. *In the following viewpoint, the authors report that the economic crisis threatens many governments. There have been protests in Britain and France, and French president Nicolas Sarkozy and British prime minister Gordon Brown are increasingly unpopular. In China, the government is attempting to quell unrest with stimulus packages and giveaways. According to the authors, Russia is moving to repress dissent in the press, but otherwise seems ill-equipped to deal with the financial crisis or the attendant fall in popular support for the government.*

As you read, consider the following questions:

1. According to the International Monetary Fund, which nation faces the worst downturn among all highly developed economies?

2. China and Russia experienced serious crises in the 1990s after they did what with their state-owned enterprises, according to the authors?

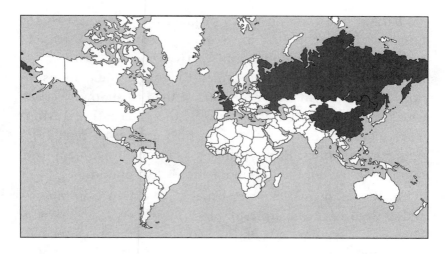

3. In December 2008, by how much did disposable income sink in Russia, as the authors report?

In the cabinet of French President Nicolas Sarkozy, there was talk of a "Black Thursday," and from Sarkozy's perspective, that was exactly what Jan. 29, 2009 turned out to be. Schools were closed, and so were railroads, banks and stock markets. Theaters, radio stations and even ski lifts were shut down temporarily. Trash receptacles were set on fire in Paris once again, and a crowd gathered on the city's famed Place de l'Opéra to sing the "Internationale," the anthem of revolution.

The Financial Crisis Sparks Protests

The global financial crisis has already reached France, bringing business failures, mass layoffs for some workers and reduced working hours for others. On that infamous Thursday, it drove up to 2.5 million people into the streets, in cities from Marseilles to Brest and Bordeaux. The situation was not like in May 1968, when France was in a state of emergency [street protests caused the collapse of the government]. Nevertheless, the country's unions called the demonstrations "historic," characterizing them as the most important protest movement to date against the current French president.

Paris is not the only place plagued by unrest. Across the English Channel in Britain, workers protested at a refinery near Immingham in Lincolnshire, triggering solidarity strikes in 19 other locations in the United Kingdom. The demonstrations became a symbol for the fears of the British lower classes, because the country—according to the International Monetary Fund—faces the worst downturn among all highly developed economies. Prime Minister Gordon Brown's approval rating is following the decline of the British pound.

In Russia, dismal labor statistics have driven Communists and anti-government protestors into the streets from Pskov to Volgograd in recent days, and in Moscow members of the left-wing opposition even ventured onto Red Square. They ripped up pictures of Prime Minister Vladimir Putin, until police arrested and removed them.

In China, workers returned from festivities marking the spring festival to hear shocking news from their own government. Beijing announced that about 20 million migrant workers—more than the combined populations of Denmark, Sweden and Norway—would likely become unemployed in the coming months. The fast pace of economic growth that has lent legitimacy to the Communist Party's hold on power until now has slowed considerably. According to a government spokesman, 2009 will be the "most difficult" year since the turn of the millennium.

About 50 million jobs could be lost worldwide in the next 11 months and more than 200 million people could drift into total poverty, warns the International Trade Union Confederation (ITUC). Guy Ryder, the group's general secretary, believes that these changes represent a "social time bomb," and that the resulting instability could become "extremely hazardous to democracy" in some countries.

In the West, the crisis could cost heads of state their jobs, as was recently the case with the prime minister of Iceland. But what does it mean for the giant countries in the East?

Could the regime in Beijing falter as the country faces its greatest challenge since the beginning of market reforms? Are the Russian people terminating their political moratorium with the government, because prices are rising while the ruble falls, or could the middle class even be about to rebel?

About 50 million jobs could be lost worldwide in the next 11 months . . . the resulting instability could become "extremely hazardous to democracy" in some countries.

Sarkozy's Popularity Falls in France

Cabinets in London, Moscow, Beijing and Paris have been overcome by a sense of helplessness. Self-confessed workaholic Gordon Brown is trying to cope with calamity by taking constant countermeasures, while Putin sends his police officers into the street and Beijing distributes gifts to the poorest of the poor. French President Sarkozy, on the other hand, remained silent for a full seven days after the first major, large-scale demonstration.

The French president, who usually seizes every possible opportunity to grab the limelight, waited an entire week before finally reacting to nationwide strikes. Last Thursday evening [February 5, 2009], on instructions from the Elysée Palace, 90 minutes of broadcast time was made available for a television interview, and Sarkozy quickly switched into propaganda offensive mode on multiple TV and radio stations. The gist of his message was that there would be no change in direction, and that the government would continue to emphasize reforms.

In light of what he dubbed a "crisis of brutal proportions," the president knowingly pointed to "hardships" and "worries" and massaged the soul of the nation with therapeutic platitudes. But that was the extent of it, because Sarkozy knows that the Jan. 29 [2009] demonstrations did not reach critical mass by a long shot. The motley alliance of protesting professors, nurses, steel workers and students lacked a shared list of economic and political demands. Their banners made a case for wage increases, purchasing power parity or the repeal of tax reforms for the rich. At the same time, however, the protests revealed a deep-seated malaise that penetrates deeply into the conservative electorate of the governing UMP [Union for a Popular Movement, a center-right political party]. The overwhelming majority of the French are plagued by fears of unemployment, lower incomes and shrinking savings.

The galloping decline in the economy has further damaged the president's standing. Now that his approval rating has dropped to only 39 percent, Sarkozy is very much on edge. After being booed by angry citizens during a visit to the normally tranquil town of Saint-Lô, the president reacted by imposing a disciplinary transfer on the town's prefect and chief of police.

The galloping decline in the economy has further damaged [French president Sarkozy's] standing. Now that his approval rating has dropped to only 39 percent, Sarkozy is very much on edge.

Two-thirds of the French believe that their government—despite the €26 billion [euros] ($34 billion) economic stimulus package, which even includes plans to renovate churches, government ministries and prisons—is not engaging in effective crisis management.

Politically speaking, the man in charge at the Elysée Palace will remain unchallenged until 2012. Sarkozy has a solid majority in both the National Assembly and the Senate. The Communists have shrunk to the point of insignificance, and the Socialists are crippled by internecine feuds. This week, however, the alliance of trade unions is discussing new battleground tactics, and it knows that it can depend on the support of the majority of French people.

"The sympathy for the strike movement highlights the ever-deepening rift between the French and their president," warns political scientist and opinion researcher Stéphane Rozès. "We are on the brink of a new epoch, one that will be marked by growing political instability."

Gordon Brown's Popularity Falls in Britain

British Prime Minister Gordon Brown's popularity is falling even faster than Sarkozy's. Despite a temporary boost last fall [2008], when Brown showed leadership strength at home and internationally with his plan to recapitalize the banks, fewer and fewer Britons are now confident that the man at 10 Downing Street [the residence of the British prime minister] has the right recipe for the crisis.

According to recent polls, the opposition Tories have further widened their lead to a comfortable 10 to 12 percent, while only one in three Britons would vote for Labour today. The drop in the approval ratings of Brown and Chancellor of the Exchequer [or Finance Minister] Alistair Darling is especially dramatic on issues of economic competence, where the pair lost a full 12 percentage points within only a month.

These are disconcerting numbers, especially for Brown's Labour party, which almost kicked the prime minister out of office last summer. Coming to grips with the public's growing anger will be one of the prime minister's most important tasks. Although Brown's smart, academic analyses against protectionism are impressive to listeners in places like Davos [Switzerland, site of the World Economic Forum], the premier is increasingly alienating concerned traditional voters like the folks in Lincolnshire.

In better times, for example, the strike in front of the Lincolnshire refinery would have elicited nothing but a shrug from most British workers. The operator of the plant, the

French energy company Total, had wanted to use 300 skilled workers from Italy and Portugal, provided by an Italian sub-contractor, for a construction project. According to the unions, the workers were being paid less than they should have been, which Total denied.

After days of unruly strikes, the parties reached an agreement last Wednesday, in which Total agreed to provide 102 additional jobs for British workers. It was a courtesy gesture by the company to preserve the peace. Under the current law, there was nothing illegal about temporarily employing the Italian and Portuguese workers.

The 102 additional jobs are the price the company paid for social peace, but whether it will last is more than questionable. "We may have won the battle, but the fight goes on," says Shaune Clarkson of the GMB union [general trade union]. No one knows whether the message has reached Brown in London, where more and more observers believe that the prime minister lost touch with the public long ago.

China Seems Stable for Now

If anyone has a receptive ear for angry grumbling in the streets, it is governments like those in Beijing and Moscow. Both China and Russia experienced serious crises in the 1990s, when their old Communist, state-owned enterprises were shut down. In China, 50 million people became unemployed within a short space of time, and in Russia the economic crash almost cost President Boris Yeltsin his reelection in 1996. But both regimes persevered, because both the Chinese and the Russians, after long years of Communist planned economies, were undemanding. But in the wake of the economic boom of recent years and the growing prosperity of large segments of the middle class, those days are over.

Ironically, in the year [2009] in which the Chinese Communist Party plans to celebrate the 60th anniversary of its rule with a great deal of pomp, the country, for the first time in a

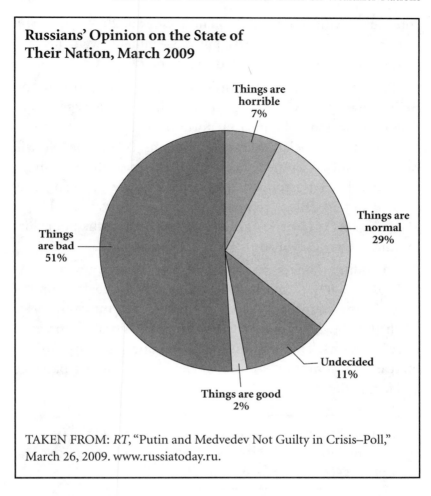

Russians' Opinion on the State of Their Nation, March 2009

Things are horrible 7%

Things are normal 29%

Things are bad 51%

Undecided 11%

Things are good 2%

TAKEN FROM: *RT*, "Putin and Medvedev Not Guilty in Crisis–Poll," March 26, 2009. www.russiatoday.ru.

long while, will not be able to boast impressive economic statistics. The economy grew by only 6.8 percent in the last quarter. To keep high school and university graduates employed, China must increase its manufacturing production or the services it provides by about 8 percent annually.

No one truly believes that Communist Party leader Hu Jintao or Premier Wen Jiabao could suffer the fate of former Indonesian President Suharto, who was swept away by the 1998 Asian economic crisis after ruling the country for more than 30 years. Nevertheless, "Chinese society will likely be confronted with more conflicts and clashes in 2009, which will test the abilities of the party and government even further," warned the government-owned magazine *Outlook*.

Preventing unrest is the order of the day, and to that end Beijing has approved an economic stimulus package worth €460 billion ($598 billion). A portion of the money is to be spent on better social insurance programs, so that people will save less and consume more. A plan to raise the minimum wage has been postponed. Nevertheless, local governments handed out so-called "red envelopes," each containing 100 to 150 yuan (€11–17 or $14–22), to the poorest of the poor during the spring festival so they can buy food.

In addition, Beijing came up with an unusual program. As of Feb. 1 [2009], farmers are receiving a cash rebate from the government equivalent to 13 percent of the purchase price when they buy television sets, washing machines, motorcycles or refrigerators. The Communist Party hopes the program will increase consumption—but also that it will buy it patience and sympathy.

Preventing unrest is the order of the day, and to that end Beijing has approved an economic stimulus package worth €460 billion ($568 billion).

The party is especially concerned about migrant workers, who are losing their jobs at a breathtaking rate. There is hardly anyone left in their native villages for farming. The tenseness of the situation is palpable in China's so-called "job markets," such as the one in Canton's Huadu district. Last week, on a side street wedged between factories, shops and apartment buildings, hundreds of men and women jostled up to tables at several leather factories that make bags for the domestic, Russian and American markets. Jobs were available—for a 10-hour day and without employment contracts.

Nevertheless, the mood in Canton still seems relaxed. And yet no one can predict how long the public's confidence will last. Those who, despite all efforts, can no longer afford the tuition to send their children to school or their parents to the doctor may eventually lose patience with the authorities. In recent weeks, several protests in front of factory gates have turned violent, with police vehicles going up in flames and workers ransacking party offices.

The party is especially concerned about students, who have rarely dared to take to the streets since the 1989 Tiananmen Square massacre. But this could change when their dreams of enjoying a successful career in return for the hard work of their student years threaten to evaporate.

Of the roughly 5.6 million Chinese who graduated from universities and technical colleges in 2008, about a million are still without work. This year, the number of graduates entering the job market will be even higher, at 6.1 million. "If you are worried, you can rest assured that I am even more worried," Premier Wen told a group of students.

Russia Prepares to Suppress Unrest

These are not the kinds of words Russians hear from their prime minister. Since the fall, when Putin was still publicly denying that the world financial crisis posed a threat to Russia, Moscow has primarily been preparing itself for one thing: to keep its own people in check if worse comes to worst.

The rulers' fear of the ruled has plagued every Russian government since the days of the czars. It suddenly reappeared when Yevgeny Gontmacher, a respected social economist, published his essay "Novocherkassk 2009," in which he warned against uprisings in the provinces. The essay alluded to the riots that broke out in the southern Russian industrial city of Novocherkassk in June 1962, following price increases. Five thousand angry workers took to the streets, and the police and army were ordered to shoot the protestors. More than 20 people died, and seven ringleaders were executed.

The mere mention of this long-suppressed drama was enough for the authorities to threaten to withdraw the license of the liberal business magazine *Vedomosti*, which had published Gontmacher's article. The magazine was accused of "incitement to extremism"—and this despite the fact that the author had held an important post under Putin.

But in taking this approach, the Kremlin merely confirmed Gontmacher's core thesis, namely that the Putin system, which increasingly emphasized central control and repression of political foes already during times of economic growth, is incapable of responding flexibly in a serious crisis. Indeed, the government reacted in panic immediately after the first demonstrations by angry merchants in Vladivostok, who were incensed over an increase in import duties for Western used cars, by portraying the protestors as the victims of foreign intelligence services.

The Putin system, which increasingly emphasized central control and repression of political foes already during times of economic growth, is incapable of responding flexibly in a serious crisis.

Pavel Verstov, a member of Putin's United Russia party until recently, can also attest to the Kremlin's helplessness. Verstov, a local journalist, had reported on suicides at the largest steel mill in Magnitogorsk, an industrial city in the Ural Mountains region. Four workers had killed themselves because they could no longer repay their debts. Hundreds of thousands of Russians are now under similar pressure, after having taken out euro or dollar loans from banks to buy houses or cars. But now that the ruble has lost 47 percent of its value against the dollar since last September, the borrowers' salaries are no longer sufficient to service their debt.

Verstov was expelled from the government party. A local party official branded him as a "troublemaker" and declared: "The security forces will take strong steps to thwart all attempts to destabilize society." He called upon his fellow party members to stand behind President Dmitry Medvedev and Prime Minister Vladimir Putin.

The fact that there have already been open calls for Putin to resign . . . shows how quickly supposedly stable power can be eroded.

The two men are still strong in the polls, with Putin's approval rating at 83 percent. However, polls conducted by the public opinion research institute Levada Center show that confidence in the government is vanishing almost as quickly as the country's financial reserves. While only 27 percent believed that the country is moving "in a wrong direction" in October 2008, that number had already risen by half by the end of December [2008]. Almost one in two citizens fears that "the government cannot effectively combat inflation and salary losses."

To bolster the banks, the ruble and heavily indebted major companies, the government has already spent a third of its once formidable foreign currency reserves. After a still-respectable economic growth figure of 5.6 percent in 2008, German Gref, a former economics minister who now heads the country's largest bank, now expects three years of recession and stagnation. "The government does not have a plan to cope with the crisis," says Gref.

Russia's Government Is Disconnected from Its People

In this situation, it is not Garry Kasparov, the leader of the extra-parliamentary opposition, who poses a threat to the Moscow power elite, because the former world chess champion has far more supporters in the West than in Russia. And Communist Party leader Gennady Zyuganov, for his part, has made his peace with the powers that be.

The real threat comes from another direction. The Kremlin fears that members of the middle class, loyal Putin supporters, will withdraw their support if the prosperity of recent years vanishes. In December alone, disposable income sank by 11.6 percent, and 5.8 million people are already officially unemployed. Arkady Dvorkovich, economic advisor to President Medvedev, believes that the unofficial figure is closer to 20 million.

So far, few have protested in Putin's giant realm. But the fact that there have already been open calls for Putin to resign—as in Vladivostok—shows how quickly supposedly stable power can be eroded.

A respected Moscow political scientist points to a dangerous disaffection between the "ruling elite" and the passive majority, warning that there are no longer any functioning relations between the country's rulers and its population, television excluded. In times like these, he says, this could prove to be devastating—and it could ruin the Putin system.

Israel Will Cut Social Programs, but Not Military Spending

Daniel Rosenberg

Daniel Rosenberg is an Israeli student, education worker, and activist for peace and social justice. In the following viewpoint, he argues that the financial crisis will hit Israel very hard. Rosenberg says that Israel has a high rate of poverty, but that in order to keep a balanced budget it will cut needed social spending. The pension system is in bad shape, Rosenberg argues, because it was privatized in 2004 and money was placed in foreign investments. In addition, unemployment is rising. According to Rosenberg, however, the military faces no cuts and will continue to spend wastefully.

As you read, consider the following questions:

1. According to Daniel Rosenberg, what percentage of Israeli citizens live below the poverty line?

2. When were Israeli pension funds privatized?

3. According to Rosenberg, where will the cuts in NGO [nongovernmental organization] funding be especially keenly felt?

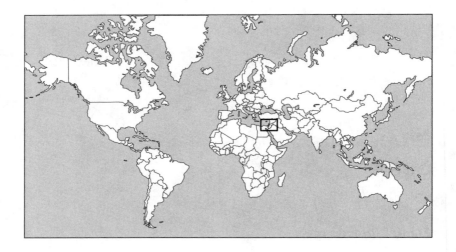

The financial crisis does not skip over Israel. The country that has been integrating itself in global capitalist markets in the last decades is once again seeing the ugliest side of capitalism, as the stock markets have dropped over a stunning 10 percent since the beginning of the month and the GDP [gross domestic product] growth forecast for the next couple of years has been slashed.

The crisis finds the Israeli society in worse shape than it was during the last recession, that of 2000–2003: currently about a quarter of Israeli citizens live below the official poverty line, among whom the percentage of minority groups, such as Israeli Arabs and Orthodox Jews, is extremely high. A large part of the Israeli poor population are defined as "working poor," meaning people who are employed and yet do not earn a minimum living wage, a phenomenon which is usually regarded as a symptom of the crumbling of the middle classes.

The Financial Crisis Will Hurt Israelis

Despite the fact that many governments around the world, from Europe to Mexico, are intending to increase spending in order to combat the oncoming recession, the Israeli government has already declared that it will keep a balanced budget and that, to do so, further cuts in social spending will be necessary. The government has not yet revealed its 2009 budget, but as in the 2003 emergency economic plan, it is likely to include reduction of state support for education and welfare, shutting down hospitals, schools, and community centers.

Despite the fact that many governments . . . are intending to increase spending . . . the Israeli government has already declared that it will keep a balanced budget and that, to do so, further cuts in social spending will be necessary.

The current crisis also has a direct effect on the pensions and long-term savings of many Israeli workers and retirees. In the last decades, Israel underwent a series of financial reforms aimed at integrating the Israeli society in the international financial system. Thus, the major pension funds, which until 1995 were held by the Israeli labor confederation, were privatized in 2004. The era also saw the acquisition of major financial institutions, such as the country's biggest insurance company and second-largest bank, by foreign holders. The financial institutions, now fully integrated in international finance, have poured investments into foreign financial markets rather than government bonds, as well as securities that enriched major Israeli tycoons, who are themselves heavily invested in foreign financial equities. The losses that the global financial sector has suffered in the last several weeks [in fall 2008] have had major impacts on the Israeli institutional investors' earnings, resulting in the pension savings shrinking by an average of 8 percent—and the worst is yet to come. Many workers, especially those nearing retirement, simply don't believe they will be able to maintain a decent standard of living, so they are forced to work in their older age.

Another sector that has been affected by the crisis is the vast network of NGOs [nongovernmental organizations] providing necessary welfare to thousands of Israelis. With the deepening poverty in Israeli society, the NGOs have come to supply many essential social services, from soup kitchens and charity to health and education. The NGOs, which often operate under the banner of "social justice," are usually heavily reliant upon contributions from wealthy Israeli and international donors, including some of the major Israeli capitalists. In times of economic turmoil, like now, donations normally become skimpier, leaving a significant part of the Israeli population without basic essentials, sometimes as basic as food and shelter. This aspect of the crisis is especially keenly felt in the Palestinian territories, as many aid programs are being cut back due to lack of funds.

Industry Faces Cuts, but the Military Does Not

The Israeli industry is also likely to suffer cutbacks; already, over 10,000 employees are expected to be fired in the next few weeks. Dependency on foreign markets, which was hailed by liberal politicians as the sign of success of the Israeli industry, is likely be its bane in times of global recession. Many venture capitalists, especially in the IT [information technology] and biotechnology sectors, are already pulling out of Israel.

However, one sector that is not showing signs of recession is the production of means of destruction. Elbit, Israel's major private arms producer, reported that its gross profit for the second quarter of 2008 increased 55.4 percent compared to the second quarter of 2007, while Magal, which specializes in security and surveillance systems, saw its revenue rising a staggering 78 percent since 2007 (Magal and Elbit are both major contractors in the building of the notorious separation wall [a barrier being built by Israel in the West Bank] in the occupied territories). Furthermore, Israel's defense budget is not likely to be cut in 2009 and will probably continue to occupy about 15 percent of the overall state expenditure. Among the billions

The Financial Crisis Has Fueled Anti-Semitism

As the financial crisis continues to affect markets around the world, anti-Semites are still using it to promote conspiracy theories about Jewish involvement in the crisis, and anti-Semitic statements and other anti-Jewish messages are appearing on a daily basis on financial Internet discussion groups and on Web sites and blogs both in the United States and abroad.

The crisis has also given birth to new anti-Semitic conspiracy theories. One of the most common rumors being circulated on the Internet suggests that, just prior to the collapse of Lehman Brothers, "$400 billion was frantically transferred to banks in Israel" by the company.

That conspiracy theory, which has no basis in fact, is reminiscent of the one that emerged immediately after the 9/11 terrorist attacks, which claimed that "4,000 Jews" did not report to work at the World Trade Center that day because they had advance warning that an attack was imminent. That Big Lie is now believed by many around the world.

Posts and public comments on financial message boards, Web sites and blogs have perpetuated anti-Semitic stereotypes and conspiracy theories alleging Jewish control of the U.S. economy, banking and government and blaming Jews for the country's financial turmoil. Some posts have gone so far as to resurrect Nazi-era propaganda with threads such as, "The Jewish Problem ... They need to be stopped ..." or comments such as, "The Final Solution 2??"

Anti-Defamation League,
"Financial Crisis Sparks Wave of Internet Anti-Semitism:
Overview," October 4, 2008. www.adl.org.

assigned to the Israeli military, $4 billion will be spent on purchasing 25 new F-35 fighters, which makes it twice as expensive as its catalogue price ($87 million apiece), to the happiness of Lockheed Martin Corporation. The government's priorities, revealed in this overpriced and needless purchase, exposes the core of Israel's geopolitical role: to be the "big stick" of US foreign policy.

Periodical Bibliography

BBC News	"Huge Crowds Join French Strikes," January 29, 2009. http://news.bbc.co.uk.
Zanny Minton Beddoes	"When Fortune Frowned," *Economist*, October 9, 2008.
David Hale, as told to Tim Harcourt	"Crunch Time—What Does the Global Financial Crisis Mean for Australia?" *Austrade*, November 12, 2008. www.austrade.gov.au.
Eben Harrell	"Corpses Pile Up amid Britain's Financial Crisis," *TIME*, October 20, 2008.
Nigel Holmes and Megan McArdle	"Iceland's Meltdown," *Atlantic*, December 2008.
Matthew Saltmarsh	"Financial Crisis Stings British Expatriates," *New York Times*, May 30, 2009.
Danny Schechter	"Financial Crisis Goes Global, Slams into Europe," *Huffington Post*, March 10, 2009. www.huffingtonpost.com.
Jay Solomon and Siobhan Gorman	"Financial Crisis May Diminish American Sway," *Wall Street Journal*, October 17, 2008.
Spiegel Online	"Ticking Timebomb: The Financial Crisis Reaches Germany's Economy," October 15, 2008. www.spiegel.de.
Brian Whitley	"With Fewer Jobs, Fewer Illegal Immigrants," *Christian Science Monitor*, December 30, 2008. www.csmonitor.com.

 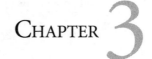

CHAPTER 3

Effects of the Global Financial Crisis on Developing Nations

Worldwide, Migrant Workers Are Threatened by Job Losses and Xenophobia

Ron Synovitz

Ron Synovitz is a senior correspondent in Radio Free Europe's central newsroom, where he has worked since 1995. In the following viewpoint, Synovitz reports that enormous numbers of migrant workers are losing their jobs in China, the Persian Gulf, and Europe. In response, governments in Spain, Russia, and elsewhere are putting restrictions on the number of foreign workers allowed into their countries. International organizations and advocacy groups worry that such restrictions on foreigners may cause dangerous large-scale migration, enrich criminal organizations by promoting illegal immigration, and encourage xenophobic attitudes toward foreigners.

As you read, consider the following questions:

1. In the Persian Gulf, from where does Ron Synovitz assert the majority of migrant workers come?

2. In Spain, where do the majority of migrant workers come from, according to the author?

3. What is the International Organization for Migration (IOM)?

For years, migrant workers from impoverished rural areas of China have flocked to factories in the country's eastern coastal areas for work.

But the global financial crisis has slowed the demand for products made in those factories. Tens of thousands have closed already this year [2008], and the number is expected to rise by year-end—leaving millions of Chinese migrants unemployed.

Already, a mass exodus is under way within China as millions of jobless migrants return from the cities to their impoverished villages.

Analysts . . . predict that as many as half of [the Persian Gulf's] 13 million foreign workers could lose their jobs in the months ahead.

Migrants in Persian Gulf and Europe Face Layoffs

In the Persian Gulf region, major construction projects financed by a seemingly endless stream of oil revenue have brought millions of migrant workers to the region—mostly from Asian countries such as India, Pakistan, Bangladesh, Sri Lanka, and the Philippines.

But now, the fall in the price of oil that has accompanied the global recession is causing a sharp downturn in development within the six Gulf Cooperation Council states—Saudi Arabia, the United Arab Emirates, Kuwait, Bahrain, Qatar, and Oman.

Analysts say neither the developers, the investors, nor the migrant workers are prepared for what is next. They predict that as many as half of the region's 13 million foreign workers could lose their jobs in the months ahead.

The migrants will either have to stay in the Gulf countries as illegal immigrants or go back to their own countries to seek employment.

European countries also are seeing similar problems as a result of the financial crisis.

Millions of foreign workers flocked to Spain for jobs from 1994 to 2007 when that country saw continuous economic growth. Most of the 4.5 million migrant workers now in Spain are from Latin America, North Africa, or Eastern Europe.

Many had jobs in construction—until this year, when the global economic crisis hit Spain's construction sector hard. In Spain, again, migrant workers have been among the first to lose their jobs.

Governments Target Foreign Workers

Complicating their situation further, the Spanish government in September announced a plan to fight soaring unemployment by limiting the number of foreign workers. Government ministers argue that they have no choice but to respond to the needs of the labor market—and protect the jobs of Spanish citizens.

UN [United Nations] Secretary-General Ban Ki-moon recently suggested that the financial crisis could uproot entire communities of foreign workers around the world and cause major changes to the dynamics of international migration.

"It would be naive to think the current [economic] crisis will have no effect on the movement of people across the borders and on how our publics perceive migration and the migrants in their midst," Ban said at a global forum in October.

"Already migration flows are reversing," he added. "In several instances, we are seeing a net outflow from countries facing economic crisis, especially from badly affected sectors such as construction and tourism, where many migrants are employed."

Ban said it is important that governments protect the rights of foreign workers in order to prevent mass migrations of angry, unemployed, and impoverished workers.

"I would also urge those countries who accommodate many migrants—they should ensure, through their domestic legislation and political and social framework—to protect and promote the human rights of migrant workers," he said.

But there are signs that the opposite is taking place in some countries.

[UN Secretary-General Ban Ki-moon] said it is important that governments protect the rights of foreign workers in order to prevent mass migrations of angry, unemployed, and impoverished workers.

In Russia, Prime Minister Vladimir Putin this month [December 2008] signed a decree aimed at reducing quotas on the number of foreigners working in the country. Putin says the move will ease the impact of the financial crisis.

But at the same time, a youth branch of Putin's United Russia party, calling itself the Young Guard, has been engaged in a campaign to reclaim jobs for Russians that are occupied by foreign migrant workers.

Andrei Tatarinov, the deputy head of Young Guard's Moscow office, . . . said the campaign aims to rid the country of "every other" migrant worker.

"Considering the difficult financial situation in our country, we believe that we must think about our native workers—take care of them, their salaries and their jobs," Tatarinov said. "We don't think it's right to feed foreign economies and send money abroad by paying migrant workers. We are ready to help the Federal Migration Service by jointly patrolling construction sites that employ many immigrants."

Governments Should Reject Xenophobia

The International Organization for Migration [IOM] is an intergovernmental organization based in Geneva, Switzerland, that works worldwide to make migration beneficial for both migrant workers and the countries involved.

Migrant Workers Face Massive Layoffs in the Persian Gulf

With property prices crashing and cranes standing motionless over abandoned construction projects on the famed Sheikh Zayed Road, Dubai has found itself in the eye of the global financial storm. Without oil revenues to provide a cushion against the downturn, the emirate finally sought a $10 billion bailout from its wealthier Emirati rival, Abu Dhabi, on February 22 [2009].

As Dubai tries to cope with its financial troubles, foreign workers are being laid off in droves, and mass deportations loom on the horizon. The growing unemployment rates for foreign workers could provide recruiting opportunities for jihadist groups in the region and further deepen social tensions for the United Arab Emirates as well as other GCC [Gulf Cooperation Council] states, which are releasing scores of blue-collar immigrant workers....

Millions of immigrants—mostly Indians, Pakistanis, Bangladeshis and Filipinos—provide the labor needed to maintain giant oil rigs and build elaborate skyscrapers in the Persian Gulf.... These demographic issues have contributed to a heated debate among Gulf political circles in the past several years over the supposed "harm" expatriate workers have inflicted on traditional Arab society. This debate takes on xenophobic and frequently racist tones.

STRATFOR, *"Gulf States: Labor Policies, Financial Crisis and Security Concerns,"* February 24, 2009. www.stratfor.com.

IOM spokesman Jean-Philippe Chauzy says that policies like those passed in Russia this month are a cause of concern for his organization as it marks International Migrants Day on December 18.

"What the International Organization for Migration is saying on International Migrants Day is that countries worldwide should recognize the positive contributions that migrants can and do make to economic growth—even at a time of global financial crisis," Chauzy says.

"And therefore, those countries should resist the temptation to close their doors to migrants in times of economic slowdown because there is a structural need for migrants," he adds.

What the International Organization for Migrants is saying . . . is that countries worldwide should recognize the positive contributions that migrants can and do make to economic growth.

Chauzy explains that government policies that close the doors to legal migration may inadvertently be enriching criminal organizations, because "policies that would tend to block migration flows will encourage more people to go through irregular routes—very often putting their lives and their savings in the hands of smuggling and trafficking networks that operate worldwide."

Perhaps most importantly, Chauzy says protectionist policies can contribute to an environment that breeds xenophobia, "because the impact of the crisis is very strong and people are competing for jobs. It would be very shortsighted of governments to start finger-pointing at migrants as being responsible for the current state of economic affairs."

In India and China, the Crisis May Worsen Poverty

Jayshree Bajoria

Jayshree Bajoria is a writer on east and south Asia at the Council on Foreign Relations (CFR). In the following viewpoint, Bajoria notes that growth in China and India has been extremely important in reducing global poverty. As the financial crisis slows that growth, poverty reduction may also slow, or even reverse. Inequality may increase, and both nations may also experience social instability. In response to the crisis, China and India have come up with a range of stimulus packages. They have also adopted some protectionist measures, which economists fear may increase, rather than decrease, poverty.

As you read, consider the following questions:

1. According to Jayshree Bajoria, what is considered to be extreme poverty?

2. After experiencing a growth rate of 9.3 percent in 2007, what does the International Monetary Fund (IMF) project India's growth rate will be in 2009?

3. In 2008, what did India's government do in response to falling global commodity prices, according to the author?

By year's end, the impact of the global financial crisis of 2008 was starting to be felt in the developing world, with slowdowns expected in all emerging economies. These growth declines could have significant effects on the world's poorest populations. The World Bank estimates that a 1 percent decline in developing country growth rates traps an additional 20 million people in poverty. Concern centers on slowing growth in India and China, the world's two most populous nations and the largest contributors to reductions in global poverty in the last two decades, according to many academic studies. Reduced economic growth in both countries could reverse poverty alleviation efforts and even push more people into poverty, say some experts. The financial crisis has also likely made the achievement of the United Nations' [UN] Millennium Development Goals (MDGs) on poverty—to halve the proportion of people in extreme poverty by 2015—more difficult.

China and India Had Success in Reducing Poverty

With an average annual growth rate of 10 percent, China has lifted over 600 million of its 1.3 billion citizens out of extreme poverty—those who earn less than $1 a day—since 1981. In the same time period, India's 6.2 percent average annual growth rate has brought an estimated 30 million out of its 1.1 billion people out of extreme poverty. But an estimated 100 million Chinese and more than 250 million Indians remained under the extreme poverty line in 2005, according to the latest World Bank poverty estimates. Roughly 470 million Chinese and 827 million Indians earned less than $2 a day, the median poverty line for all developing countries. Though some economists say World Bank figures understate the true extent of poverty, there is broad agreement that a slowdown in China and India will harm poverty alleviation goals. The administrator of the UN Development Programme (UNDP), Kemal Dervis, warned in October 2008 that together with volatile food and fuel prices, "current global economic conditions threaten the gains that have been made to reduce poverty and advance development for large numbers of people."

There is broad agreement that a slowdown in China and India will harm poverty alleviation goals.

In the developing world as a whole, economists say that soaring food and fuel prices were already placing strain on the poor prior to the onset of the financial crisis. The UN World Food Programme estimated in September 2008 that there are 850 million chronically hungry people in the world, a tally that could increase by 130 million this year. The World Bank estimates that the number of poor increased by at least 100 million as a result of the food and fuel crises. It argues that declines in food and fuel prices in late 2008 have not solved the problem. According to its November 2008 report, the poorest households were "forced to switch from more expensive to cheaper and less nutritional foodstuffs, or cut back on total calorie intake altogether, face weight loss and severe malnutrition."

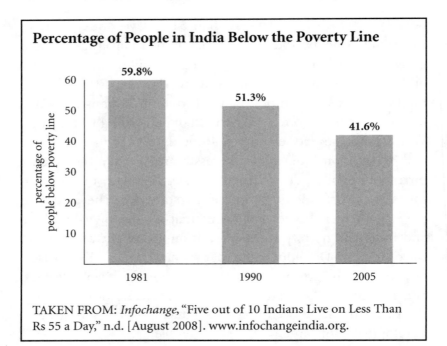

Percentage of People in India Below the Poverty Line

TAKEN FROM: *Infochange*, "Five out of 10 Indians Live on Less Than Rs 55 a Day," n.d. [August 2008]. www.infochangeindia.org.

The poor in India and China, like the rest of the world, have also been affected by the rise in fuel and food prices. For India the problem is especially vexing. The 2008 Global Hunger Index of the International Food Policy Research Institute says India already suffers from alarming levels of hunger, and is one of three countries with the highest prevalence—more than 40 percent—of underweight children under five.

Inequality in China and India May Increase

The financial crisis could worsen the existing high levels of inequality in China and India, say experts. . . . Despite unprecedented levels of economic growth in India and China, there is increasing geographic, sector-based, and income inequalities within each country. Benefits from growth have failed to trickle down to significant segments of each population, especially in rural areas. Biplove Choudhary of the UNDP's trade program says growth does not directly translate into poverty alleviation. Experts say gains from growth in India and China should be better channeled into areas that most uplift the rural poor, such as spending on health, education, and infrastructure.

Yet sharply tighter credit conditions and weaker growth are likely to cut into governments' abilities to invest to meet education, health, and gender goals, hitting the poor the hardest, says the World Bank. An October 2008 report on global income inequality by the International Labour Organization [ILO] says income inequality, on the rise in most regions of the world, is expected to increase due to the global financial crisis.

Social unrest could spike if China's annual growth rate falls below 8 percent.

China, with its current account surplus [trade surplus] and nearly $2 trillion in foreign reserves, is better placed than India to continue long-term investments in infrastructure and social-welfare initiatives. In November 2008, the *Wall Street Journal* reported that as many as half of India's planned highway improvement projects, valued at more than $6 billion, could be delayed as much as two years. India is especially hard-hit, it says, because it had expected private investments to fund around half of the more than $100 billion a year in planned infrastructure development.

Instability in China and India May Increase

Falling employment and increasing poverty levels may precipitate political and social troubles in India and China. For more than two decades, China's Communist Party has used economic reforms as a source of legitimacy for its rule, even as it resists political freedoms and tries to rein in dissidents in the autonomous regions of Xinjiang and Tibet. But if a decline in growth slows the rate of economic reforms, it could threaten the party, say experts. CFR [Council on Foreign Relations] International Affairs Fellow Brian P. Klein writes in the *Far Eastern Economic Review* that social unrest could spike if China's annual growth rate falls below 8 percent, a level of growth inadequate to create the number of new jobs required.

A slowdown in exports contributed to the closing of at least 67,000 factories across China in the first half of 2008, prompting laid-off workers to take to the streets in protest. Joshua Kurlantzick of the Carnegie Endowment for International Peace's China program writes in the *New Republic* that so far China has kept the labor protests separate from one another, preventing them from developing a common theme or a common leader. "But if China's downturn turns into an outright recession, the country could face its first serious threat to the regime," he warns.

According to the International Monetary Fund's (IMF) 2008 world economic outlook, China's gross domestic product (GDP) growth is expected to fall from 11.9 percent in 2007 to 9.3 percent in 2009. Adam Segal, CFR senior fellow for China studies, says the Chinese government's announcement of a $586 billion stimulus package in November 2008 shows how worried leaders are. "This is the first serious slowdown for China in thirty years," he says, adding that the government knows that to maintain social stability, it must keep generating employment for those migrating from rural to urban areas. In an October 2008 meeting with Singapore's prime minister, Chinese President Hu Jintao acknowledged the need for sustained economic reforms. He said the country will sustain its economic and social stability by "transforming the economic growth pattern, restructuring the economy, attaching more importance to agriculture, and taking regulatory measures."

In India, no one is going to be satisfied with a growth rate lower than what they have come to expect in the last ten years, says Arvind Subramanian, a senior fellow at the Peterson Institute for International Economics. The IMF projects India's growth will fall from 9.3 percent in 2007 to 6.9 percent in 2009. "Not meeting expectations poses a problem for policy," he says, adding that the government is sensitive to this and has already cut interest rates and pumped liquidity into its capital markets to sustain investment. But in India, the threat is different than the one faced by China, says Segal. India, a diverse, multiethnic, multifaith country, has always struggled with a degree of social instability as various minority groups seek redress against discrimination. Instability may rise as the country goes to the polls early next year [2009] and opposition groups try to take advantage of the financial crisis to highlight the government's deficiencies, say experts.

China's top-down governance structure gives it a greater ability to mobilize resources and implement policies faster, say experts.

China and India Are Implementing Stimulus Policies

Some economists say both China and India, with their relatively insulated financial sectors, are better positioned than many other developing economies for a quick recovery from the current crisis. The governments in both countries have responded with a slew of measures. India has undertaken a balancing act of easing the central bank's key lending rate to increase liquidity [cash flow] in the markets while moving to tighten monetary policy in other areas to stave off inflation. China, with its focus on economic growth, has announced several stimulus policies. The biggest by far is a $586-billion package slated for investment over the next two years in a number of sectors, including low-income housing, rural infrastructure, water, electricity, transportation, technological innovation, and earthquake reconstruction. Analysts see this as a step in the right direction.

China's top-down governance structure gives it a greater ability to mobilize resources and implement policies faster, say experts. CFR's Segal says "it's probably better to be a poor person in China than India" because of China's ability to spend on projects that could provide immediate relief to the poor. In India, taking steps through a democratic system makes the response time longer in such a crisis. India also lacks the ability China has to respond with direct cash transfers.

Some economists are worried about the impact on poverty reduction if the current financial crisis spurs protectionism, undermining free trade policies. In November 2008, the Indian government, in response to a fall in global commodity prices, imposed a 5 percent import duty on a range of iron and steel products, and slapped a 20 percent duty on crude soybean oil imports to protect domestic producers. India and China have also been called upon to agree to the World Trade Organization's Doha development agenda, [current trade negotiation round that began in 2001] dealing with a range of international trade reforms, including some in the agricultural sector. In July 2008, the seven-year negotiations reached a stalemate when India and China refused to compromise over measures to protect farmers in developing countries from greater liberalization of trade. But leaders attending the G-20 [a group of finance ministers and central bank governors from 20 countries] summit on the financial crisis in November 2008, which included India and China, promised to refrain from protectionist measures in the next year, and called for each country in the group to make "positive contributions" to a successful conclusion of the Doha round.

China Could Use the Crisis to Become a Responsible World Power

Jing Men

Jing Men is the InBev-Baillet Latour Chair of European Union-China Relations at the College of Europe. She is also an assistant professor of International Affairs at the Vesalius College, Brussels. In this viewpoint, Jing Men investigates how the economic crisis has enhanced China's importance in the world economy. She also states that China would be better off working with—rather than trying to compete against—the United States. Jing Men further believes that China should focus on its own economic development.

As you read, consider the following questions:

1. Since the 1970s, China's economy has grown annually by what percentage rate?
2. With what does the head of the People's Bank of China think a new world reserve currency will help?
3. What leads China's development?

The 20th century was the century of the United States. Will the 21st century be the one of China?

China is rising. Since its reform policy at the end of the 1970s, China's economy has been growing at an average rate

Jing Men, "World Financial Crisis: What It Means for Security," *NATO Review*, May 2009. Copyright © *NATO Review*, 2009. Reproduced by permission.

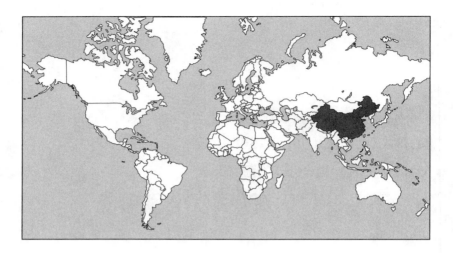

of 9 percent annually. China has become the third largest world economy. It overtook the United States as Japan's largest trading partner in 2004, as India's in 2008, and as Brazil's in 2009. China is the largest source of US imports, with which it enjoyed a trade surplus of $266.3 billion in 2008. In the same year, China became the largest foreign owner of American government debt, overtaking Japan.

Zhou Xiaochuan, the head of the People's Bank of China, feels that the flaws in the international monetary system could be dealt with to a certain degree by creating a new world reserve currency.

The financial crisis has further enhanced China's importance in the world economy. It is said to have about $2 trillion in foreign currency reserves. This huge reserve of US currency contrasts sharply with the US, whose budget deficit is likely to exceed $2 trillion this year [2009].

The Chinese government's $586 billion stimulus package demonstrated its determination to keep the crisis at bay. The Chinese Premier Wen [Jiabao] said in early 2009 that China would introduce a second stimulus package to boost its economy if necessary. The G-20 [a group of 19 industrialized nations and the European Union] summit indicated that China is expected to play a bigger role in dealing with the crisis.

China Looks to Avoid Financial Crisis in the Future

Chinese leaders are not only trying to find solutions for the problems that have occurred, but are also interested in finding out why they occurred in the first place, so as to avoid similar problems in the future.

Zhou Xiaochuan, the head of the People's Bank of China, feels that the flaws in the international monetary system could be dealt with to a certain degree by creating a new world reserve currency. His controversial idea alarmed the Americans, but was quietly welcomed by many Europeans and Asians. Although Zhou's idea is not to replace the dominant status of the dollar in the near future, it may provoke a revolution in the international monetary system.

Together with China's rising economic power, China has also steadily increased its military expenditure, with double digit annual growth. It is building its military force into one which matches its rising economic power and which can defend, in particular, its air and sea territory. After many years of discussion among its leaders, China will probably have its first aircraft carrier in the coming years.

As a consequence of its military build up, China has gradually flexed its muscle and become more active. For the first time since the Ming Dynasty, China sent ships to protect its vessels when two of its destroyers and a supply ship were sent to an area off the Somalian coast. China has also carried out several military exercises with other members of the Shanghai Cooperation Organisation [SCO].

China Continues to Hold Back

[The G20, a group of 19 industrialized nations and the European Union] backed $1.1 trillion in International Monetary Fund [IMF] financing [in its April 2009 meeting] ...

But China's part in the package appeared limited in relation to its size as perhaps the world's second-largest economy after the United States. ...

China ... has so far committed only $40 billion to the new IMF program. ... That compares with specific pledges of $100 billion each from the United States, the European Union, and Japan.

"China consistently plays well under its weight," said Gary Hufbauer, senior fellow at the Peterson Institute for International Economics in Washington.

Michael Lelyveld, "China's G-20 Role Debated,"
Radio Free Asia Online, *April 13, 2009, www.rfa.org*

Since early 2009, there have been several reports that Chinese vessels have harassed alleged American spying ships in the South China Sea. In June, a Chinese submarine accidentally collided with an underwater sonar array towed by an American destroyer which was in the South China Sea to participate in a joint military exercise with ASEAN [Association of Southeast Asian Nations] members.

Crisis Could Be an Opportunity

Most recently, the BRIC (Brazil, Russia, India, China) countries held their first summit meeting. Seeing the international crisis as an opportunity for the international economic and political order to be readjusted, the four countries expressed their ambition and willingness to participate more actively in international affairs. China is undoubtedly the most influential among the four, but the BRIC format can be a good platform for China to bargain with the US and Europe on issues of sustainable development, global warming and world peace and stability.

Some people have postulated that the role of the United States in the global economy is declining, with its position as a world leader being replaced by China. The financial crisis seems to give China a golden opportunity to strengthen this trend. But, while it is undeniable that there is a long term tendency that China is rising, the current financial crisis will not dramatically facilitate China's rise at the sacrifice of the interests of the United States.

Why not? First of all, the financial crisis is a challenge for both the US and China. The fact that China is the largest owner of US debt only serves to emphasise that the two are in the same boat. Both must accept this major interdependence and coordinate with each other. And like it or not, China will be obliged to continue to buy American debt.

Beijing faces huge pressure to maintain the 8 percent growth rate of its GDP [gross domestic product], because failure to do so would bring huge social problems.

Although the Chinese Premier Wen expressed his concern early this year about the value of the American debt, he knows that if China stopped buying it, its value would drop even more drastically. China needs to help the United States in order to help itself. On the other hand, while China is in search of other currencies as target of investment, it seems that neither euros nor yens are ready to serve as alternatives.

Furthermore, China's development is led by exports. The drastic decline of demand from the United States, the European Union and Japan due to financial crisis had an immediate impact on Chinese foreign trade—it decreased 25.9 percent in May 2009 compared to the same period of the previous year. Many export-oriented enterprises have been bankrupted and more than 20 million workers have become jobless.

Long-Term Development Remains a Challenge for China

The financial crisis posed questions to the Chinese government: how to effectively stimulate domestic consumption? How to create jobs for the laid-off workers? How to maintain sustainable development? Beijing faces huge pressure to maintain the 8 percent growth rate of its GDP, because failure to do so would bring huge social problems. Even if the problems are solved in the short term, the problem of sustainable development in the long run will remain a challenge for the Chinese government.

China will need to address lagging political and social reform in order to build up a comprehensive welfare system which offers its people reasonable social security. Only by removing Chinese people's concerns about education, medical insurance and pensions can domestic consumption be stimulated effectively. But this will not happen overnight.

Finally and most importantly, China has neither the ambition nor the capability to challenge the leadership of the United States. Compared with the superpower of the US, China is only a regional power. Both the cost and risk are too high for Beijing to commit itself to so many international issues as the US, from Iraq to Afghanistan, from Iran to North Korea.

More power in the world means more responsibility. But China is not yet ready to take on so much international responsibility. China's top priority is its own economic development. What China cares about most is regional peace and stability. Despite the fact that China is rising, it is incapable of playing the role the United States has been playing in international affairs.

In fact, the economic and political order established by the United States created a favourable environment for China's development. China jumped on the bandwagon of the US and benefited tremendously from the international system maintained by the US. The benefits Beijing gains will encourage it to stay under the leadership of Washington.

If managed well, China's both hard power and soft power will further grow after the financial crisis—but the US's will still be unmatched. What China needs to clarify to the US is that they are not competitors but partners—for both their own interests and those of the world.

The Philippines Is in a Good Position to Weather the Crisis

Antonio A. Esguerra II

Antonio A. Esguerra II is an economic development specialist at the Philippines' National Economic and Development Authority (NEDA). In the following viewpoint, he says that, relative to other nations, the Philippine banking system and the economy as a whole have not been badly hit by the financial crisis. Nonetheless, the Philippine government has taken precautions, setting aside emergency funds, increasing deposit insurance, increasing spending, lowering taxes, and pushing through other reforms.

As you read, consider the following questions:

1. According to the central bank of the Philippines, the Bangko Sentral ng Pilipinas (BSP), what percentage of the Philippine banking system was invested in Lehman Brothers?

2. As Antonio A. Esguerra II reports, did growth in the Philippines slow at all from 2007 to 2008?

3. In the proposed 2009 Philippine budget, which sector of the economy will see increased outlays of 20 percent?

Antonio A. Esguerra II, "How the Philippines Copes with the Global Financial Crisis," Devpulse, November 13, 2008. Copyright © 2008 National Economic and Development Authority. Reproduced by permission.

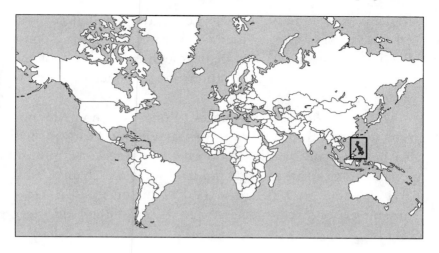

In the midst of falling stock indices, tight liquidity, low investor confidence and failing financial institutions, the International Monetary Fund [IMF] has described the current financial crisis as the "largest financial shock since the Great Depression."

While it initially reared its ugly head on Wall Street, analysts believe it has now begun to spread to the real economy, threatening the growth prospects of people on Main Street. Worse, its effects are being felt not just in the United States, but in other parts of the world as well, including the Philippines.

Philippine Banks Are Stable

The Bangko Sentral ng Pilipinas (BSP) [the Philippine central bank] said that some local banks had around US$386 million of investments in Lehman Brothers, one of the investment houses that failed as a result of the crisis. It pointed out, however, that this amount represents less than one percent of the entire banking system.

It said that key performance indicators showed sustained strength of banks' balance sheets, continued asset expansion and a growing deposit base. There are likewise no apparent problems with liquidity, [access to cash] as evidenced by a 24.1 percent year-on-year increase in bank lending in August [2008], up from the 23.9 percent growth in July. Bulk of the growth came from loans for production activities which grew by 19.8 percent.

The steady flow of remittances [money sent home by migrant workers] from OFWs [Overseas Filipino Workers] has also helped stabilize the economy by driving consumption growth and ensuring a steady influx of foreign exchange. It hit US$14.5 billion in 2007 from US$12.7 billion in 2006. Government expects remittances to hit US$17 billion this year [2008].

Key performance indicators showed sustained strength of banks' balance sheets, continued asset expansion and a growing deposit base.

In addition, government's fiscal position has been improving. "The budget deficit fell to PhP12.4 billion [Philippine pesos] in 2007 from PhP187 billion in 2004 while public sector accounts have posted surpluses in recent quarters, thanks largely to fiscal reform measures such as the Expanded Value-Added Tax law [which increased a type of sales tax]," said Socioeconomic Planning Secretary Ralph Recto.

Recto explained that fiscal reforms, effective monetary management and sound macroeconomic policies enabled the economy to post a record 7.2 percent GDP [gross domestic product] growth in 2007. With the onset of the multiple crises plaguing the international market, however, growth has slowed to 4.6 percent in the first half of this year.

The economy's performance may have slowed, but it is nonetheless respectable considering that other countries in the region also suffered a slowdown. "Economic growth in the Philippines as well as those of Asian neighbors was dragged down by high inflation and slower growth among advanced economies, which hurt consumer demand. The slowdown is more pronounced in Singapore which only posted 2.1 percent this quarter from 9.1 percent in the same period last year. Hong Kong also posted 4.2 percent growth from 6.2 percent in the same quarter last year," Recto said. For this year, government expects growth to hit 4.1 percent.

The Government Is Monitoring the Crisis

A Standard & Poor's [financial services company] official recently said that the Philippines remains "an island of calm" amid the global financial crisis, but government continues to be on alert.

To soften the impact of the global financial crisis on the poor, President Gloria Arroyo set aside PhP4.5 billion from VAT [value-added tax] collections for "pro-poor" employment and livelihood programs.

The Philippines remains "an island of calm" amid the global financial crisis, but government continues to be alert.

Malacañang [residence of the president of the Philippines] has likewise partnered with the private sector to set up a PhP100 billion "crisis fund" to finance projects that will further protect the country from the global crisis. Under the President's proposal, half of the fund will be raised by government while the other half will be shouldered by the private sector.

Recto, who is also director-general of the National Economic and Development Authority, clarified that the fund will not be used to rescue ailing financial institutions like what the US did in September [2008]. He said the amount will be used as standby funds that will be tapped for future pump-priming projects.

The Philippines' Economy Struggles as the Crisis Continues

Three months into 2009, eight of the country's top ten export destinations—including the US, its main trading partner—are in recession. As a result, the Philippine government has been forced to revise its forecast for 2009 downward from a range of 3.7–4.7 percent to 3.7–4.4 percent. Other predictions are worse—ranging from 3.8 percent by the Development Bank of Singapore to 1.8 percent by the Union Bank of Switzerland.

New year-on-year data for January 2009 underscored the dimming economic prospects. Exports dropped by 41 percent after falling sharply in December [2008] by 40 percent.

Dante Pastrana, "Rising Unemployment and Poverty in the Philippines," World Socialist.org, April 6, 2009. www.wsws.org.

Government also proposed increasing the maximum deposit insurance amount to PhP1 million from PhP250,000 for three years as a preemptive measure. If it pushes through, 98.4 percent of all deposit accounts will be covered by insurance, compared with the current level of 95.1 percent.

The Department of Labor and Employment has likewise come up with a contingency plan for OFWs that could be displaced by the crisis. The plan involves helping affected OFWs find alternative livelihood or employment opportunities in the country, as well as assisting those who still wish to work abroad.

The Government Will Increase Spending

The proposed 2009 budget, if approved, will increase overall spending by 15 percent and outlays in infrastructure by 20 percent.

Under the Comprehensive and Integrated Infrastructure Program for 2008 to 2010, the transport sector has the highest investment share at 38 percent or PhP755 billion out of the PhP2 trillion total investments. In the transport sector, roads and bridges and rail transport, with 44 percent and 39 percent of the pie, respectively, comprise the biggest share.

Aside from infrastructure, the big winners will also be social services such as education and health.

On the supply side, government has passed a law that exempts minimum wage earners from the income tax so they can have more to spend on food and education. Corporate income tax rates will also fall from 35 to 30 percent starting 2009 to encourage businesses to expand and create more jobs.

Aside from spending, the absorptive capacity of government agencies [their ability to absorb new technological information] will also be increased. The national government will also improve its coordination with local government units to make sure that infrastructure projects go to where they are needed the most. Trade, investment and tourism with other emerging markets, particularly China and the oil-rich Arab economies, will also be expanded.

Government has passed a law that exempts minimum wage earners from the income tax so they can have more to spend on food and education.

For the next two years, Recto summarized strategic investments needed to boost growth in HEARTS, meaning Health, Education, Agriculture, Roads/Bridges/Railroads, Technology/Tourism and Security/Shelter/Social Protection/Subsidies, with a focus on R for infrastructure investments.

As the world continues to suffer from a financial contagion, governments around the world are doing everything they can to end the crisis. Aside from that, they are also taking stock of the events of the past year to identify reform measures that need to be enacted, and make sure that a similar crisis won't happen again in the future.

Thankfully, the Philippines has done its homework and is in a better position to weather the global economic storm. Despite that, government along with other stakeholders remain on alert, and will continue to do so until this crisis finally reaches a decisive end.

Latin America Is Struggling to Deal with the Crisis

Woodrow Wilson International Center for Scholars

The Woodrow Wilson International Center for Scholars is a nonpartisan institute for advanced study that brings preeminent thinkers to Washington. In the following viewpoint, the center reports on a meeting of Latin American experts. Speakers at the meeting point out that growth in the region has halted and that poverty and middle-class hardship are likely to increase. The center also suggests that while some nations in Latin America have pursued responsible economic policies, others such as Nicaragua and Venezuela have not and may now experience instability. Despite possible turmoil, speakers note, the region is much more politically stable overall than in the past.

As you read, consider the following questions:

1. According to Rebeca Grynspan, how many working poor people are there likely to be in Latin America in 2009?

2. According to Arturo Porzecanski, which countries are part of the "responsible left and right"?

3. When was the last military coup in Latin America, according to Jorge I. Domínguez?

Woodrow Wilson International Center for Scholars, "The Global Financial Crisis: Implications for Latin America," A summary of an event hosted by the Latin American Program, Harvard University's David Rockefeller Center for Latin American Studies and the Council of the Latin Americas/Americas Society at Woodrow Wilson International Center for Scholars on Febuary 5, 2009. Copyright © 2009, The Woodrow Wilson International Center for Scholars. All rights reserved. Reproduced by permission.

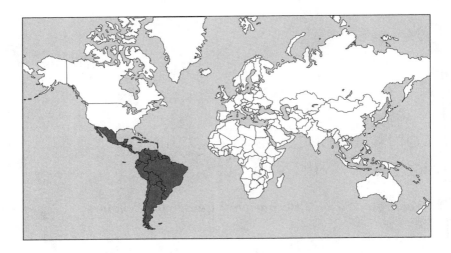

Until mid-2008, Latin American countries appeared well-equipped to weather a burgeoning economic crisis in the United States and elsewhere and emerge relatively unscathed. Solid levels of economic growth, sound fiscal and monetary policies, lower levels of debt, and stronger reserves due to high commodity prices caused many to believe that Latin America had successfully "de-coupled" its economic future from the fate of the United States and other advanced industrial countries. By September 2008, the full impact of the financial meltdown in the United States had begun to be felt in Latin America. On February 5, 2009, the Latin American Program joined with the Harvard University's David Rockefeller Center for Latin American Studies and the Americas Society/Council of the Americas [AS/COA] to explore the economic, social, and political implications of the global financial crisis for the countries of the region.

The Crisis Has Halted Growth

In a keynote address, Pamela Cox, World Bank vice president for Latin America and the Caribbean, acknowledged much uncertainty about how to respond to a crisis the scope of which has never been seen in the lifetime of most economists.

Already, the crisis has brought to a "screeching halt" five years of economic growth in Latin America; forecasts for growth rates in 2009 plunged from 3.7 percent in September 2008 to 1 percent in December, with some economies likely to experience negative growth. She called for timely, decisive action to protect the social gains of the last several years and to prevent the financial crisis from becoming a human and social one. Cox suggested an increase in support to the most vulnerable—although not just the very poor—through well-targeted social protection packages to ensure broad access to health insurance, protect public spending in key areas such as nutrition and vaccines, and expand existing conditional cash transfer programs. Allowing that there is much debate over the role of the state and the balance between public and private sector initiatives, she urged governments not to unduly cut budgets and to maintain policies aimed at long-term growth, such as investments in infrastructure and quality education. To bolster the labor market, she suggested public works programs and initiatives supporting self-employment and micro-enterprise development. The World Bank will be increasing both grants and concessional loans over the next three years to meet these challenges. Cox noted that trade wars during the Great Depression contributed to a global downward spiral, and said that the April 2009 Summit of the Americas provided a regional opportunity to emphasize the importance of open trade.

Director for the United Nations Development Programme's Bureau for Latin America and the Caribbean Rebeca Grynspan discussed the crisis's social implications, noting that not just overall growth but per capita income was declining. Inequality and poverty remain high throughout the region, and a key weakness of the region's economies is the heavy dependence on commodity income. The overall impact of the crisis will depend on how long it lasts, how governments behave, and how the international community responds to Latin America.

Currently, she said, 85 million people receive subsidies through targeted conditional cash transfer programs, but the state cannot be seen to be working only on behalf of the poor. The middle class is also suffering, and a large population goes back and forth above and below the poverty line. The International Labour Organization estimates that the number of people living in "work poverty"—those active in the labor market but earning an income below the poverty line established by the World Bank—will rise from 6.8 percent in 2007 to 8.7 percent in 2009, constituting 7 million working poor. An additional 4 million people will lose their jobs in 2009 if growth rates, as projected, are only around 1 percent. Grynspan argued for a larger system of social protection to prevent huge reversals of the gains in reducing poverty in recent years. Programs should emphasize women and young people, who are twice as likely to be unemployed, while infrastructure investment should include small and community-based projects, not just large-scale ones. In 2009–10 over a dozen elections will be held in Latin America. The middle class and residents in urban areas, not just the poor, will determine the outcomes.

Forecasts for growth rates in 2009 plunged from 3.7 percent in September 2008 to 1 percent in December, with some economies likely to experience negative growth.

Different Nations Will Feel Different Effects

Arturo Porzecanski, distinguished economist-in-residence at American University's School of International Service, emphasized the crisis's different impacts across Latin America, and divided the region into three groups with different levels of ability to respond to or cushion the crisis. The first group consists of countries such as Mexico, Central America, and the Caribbean, which depend on the United States and Europe as export markets, sources of workers' remittances, and tourism

The Crisis Is Reducing Mexican Emigration

Mexico City's ... [National Institute of Statistics and Geography] recently reported that from August 2007 to August 2008, the illegal and legal outflow of migrants has declined by over 50 percent, from 455,000 to 204,000. Additionally, remittances—the funds sent from immigrants abroad to their families at home—have decreased for the first time since 1995. The number of Mexican households receiving money from relatives abroad, largely in the United States, has fallen from 1.41 million in 2005 to 1.16 million in 2008. Remittances themselves, second only to oil as Mexico's largest source of foreign income, have decreased by 11.6 percent to $1.57 billion from January 2008 to January 2009...

Although this decrease is less than that which the Banco de México forecasted, the financial crisis paints a bleak future for the Mexican economy, whose expected negative growth of 0.8–1.8 percent would represent the sharpest decline since that of 7 percent in 1995.

Edward W. Littlefield,
"As Mexico's Problems Mount: The Impact of the
Economic Recession on Migration Patterns from Mexico,"
Council on Hemispheric Affairs, March 5, 2009. www.coha.org.

revenue. A second group consists of the "irresponsible left" of Nicaragua, Venezuela, Ecuador, Argentina, and Bolivia, whose governments have spent most of the bonanza from five years of sustained growth and do not have entries into the capital markets or good relations with foreign investors; unless commodity prices recover, these countries will be under tremendous pressure internally. A third group is made up of the "responsible left and right"—Colombia, Peru, Chile, Uruguay, and Brazil—where governments have saved some of the windfall of recent years, have more credible central banks, flexible exchange rates, and a greater ability to apply counter-cyclical fiscal and monetary policies and manage liability.

In signaling a new approach, President [Barack] Obama has made clear that the United States does not have all the answers and can learn from the experience of regional leaders.

Jorge I. Domínguez, Antonio Madero Professor of Mexican and Latin American Politics and Economics at Harvard University, noted a number of positive political developments in the region, including the absence of military coups since 1976 and the spread of civilian, constitutional, elected government. In the "old Latin America," he said, one would have expected a coup in Argentina as a result of the economic crisis in 2000–02. Current leaders (with the exception of presidents in Mexico, Colombia, and El Salvador) have for the most part been less market-oriented than their predecessors, but public opinion has not shown a left-right divide on such critical issues as citizen security, trade, and abortion. Indeed, the only issue on which an ideological left-right divide mattered appeared to be on attitudes toward the [George W.] Bush administration. Domínguez described five voting cycles in Latin America since the transitions to democracy began 30 years ago. These cycles show patterns of defeat and victory for incumbents only partially correlated with economic trends (incumbents tended to win in South America since the early 2000s, a period of macroeconomic stability and the commodity boom.) The circulation of elites serves democracy well, he observed, and even leaders who have governed well are likely to lose in coming years as a result of the recession.

The United States Hopes to Work with the Region

Robert King, acting senior director for Western Hemisphere Affairs at the National Security Council, said that the new administration was still in the process of determining what it wanted to accomplish in Latin America and how to follow through regarding principles laid out during the campaign. Overarching goals—to advance democracy, economic opportunity and security—are likely to remain unchanged, although the new president has emphasized in discussions with several Latin American presidents the importance of working together in partnership. In signaling a new approach, President [Barack] Obama has made clear that the United States does not have all the answers and can learn from the experience of regional leaders. A top priority is to work toward energy security in Latin America, and both energy and climate change are critical areas of future U.S.-Latin America cooperation. The upcoming Summit of the Americas will provide an opportunity to unveil new initiatives. The administration is committed to expanding trade benefits to all countries, and will increase the emphasis on the labor and environmental provisions of trade agreements. There is also a desire to advance opportunity from the bottom up as well as to substantially increase aid to the region.

Islamic Banks Are Insulated from the Crisis

Faiza Saleh Ambah

Faiza Saleh Ambah is a Saudi journalist who writes for the Washington Post. In the following viewpoint, she reports that Islamic banks must follow sharia, or Islamic law, which prohibits the charging of interest or trading in debt. All bank funds must be invested in actual productive enterprises. This means that Islamic banks do not use complicated financial instruments or take excessive risks, and their returns are never very large. But it also means that they avoided the financial bubble and the collapse that have devastated Western banking.

As you read, consider the following questions:

1. Besides government regulators, what group must Islamic banks please, according to the author?
2. When does the author assert modern Islamic banking began?
3. What is the name of the commercial paper providing predetermined returns that is issued by Islamic banks?

Jiddah, Saudi Arabi—As big Western financial institutions have teetered one after the other in the crisis of recent weeks, another financial sector is gaining new confidence: Islamic banking.

Proponents of the ancient practice, which looks to sharia law for guidance and bans interest and trading in debt, have been promoting Islamic finance as a cure for the global financial meltdown.

This week, Kuwait's commerce minister, Ahmad Baqer, was quoted as saying that the global crisis will prompt more countries to use Islamic principles in running their economies. U.S. Deputy Treasury Secretary Robert M. Kimmitt, visiting Jiddah, said experts at his agency have been learning the features of Islamic banking.

Though the trillion-dollar Islamic banking industry faces challenges with the slump in real estate and stock prices, advocates say the system has built-in protection from the kind of runaway collapse that has afflicted so many institutions. For one thing, the use of financial instruments such as derivatives, blamed for the downfall of banking, insurance and investment giants, is banned. So is excessive risk-taking.

"The beauty of Islamic banking and the reason it can be used as a replacement for the current market is that you only promise what you own. Islamic banks are not protected if the economy goes down—they suffer—but you don't lose your shirt," said Majed Al-Refai, who heads Bahrain-based Unicorn Investment Bank.

The beauty of Islamic banking and the reason it can be used as a replacement for the current market is that you only promise what you own.

The theological underpinning of Islamic banking is scripture that declares that collection of interest is a form of usury, which is banned in Islam. In the modern world, that translates into an attitude toward money that is different from that found in the West: Money cannot just sit and generate more money. To grow, it must be invested in productive enterprises.

"In Islamic finance you cannot make money out of thin air," said Amr Al-Faisal, a board member of Dar Al-Maal Al-Islami, a holding company that owns several Islamic banks and financial institutions. "Our dealings have to be tied to actual economic activity, like an asset or a service. You cannot make money off of money. You have to have a building that was actually purchased, a service actually rendered, or a good that was actually sold."

In the Western world, bankers designing investment instruments have to satisfy government regulators. In Islamic banking, there is another group to please—religious regulators called a sharia board. Finance lawyers work closely with Islamic finance scholars, who study and review a product before issuing a fatwa, or ruling, on its compliance with sharia law.

Islamic bankers describe depositors as akin to partners—their money is invested, and they share in the profits or, theoretically, the losses that result. (In interviews, bankers couldn't recall a case in which depositors actually lost money; this shows that banks put such funds only in very low-risk investments, they said.)

Rather than lend money to a home buyer and collect interest on it, an Islamic bank buys the property and then leases it to the buyer for the duration of the loan. The client pays a set amount each month to the bank, then at the end obtains full ownership. The payments are structured to include the cost of the house, plus a predetermined profit margin for the bank.

In interviews, bankers couldn't recall a case in which depositors actually lost money; this shows that banks put such funds only in very low-risk investments, they said.

Sharia-compliant institutions also cannot invest in alcohol, pornography, weapons, gambling, tobacco or pork.

Computer engineer Tarek Al-Bassam said the crisis made him glad that he had chosen an Islamic bank to take his money. His Islamic savings account has made about 4 percent profit, he said. "Usually it's a very low risk or a very low gain. But I'm happy with it," Bassam said.

He has also borrowed from an Islamic bank, to buy a building. Even if he's late in his payments, he said, he will not have to pay cumulative interest or a larger sum than the one agreed upon. But he notes that under this system, it can be harder to get a loan than from a conventional bank. Islamic banks have stricter lending rules and require that their borrowers provide more collateral and have higher income.

Islamic banking has grown by about 15 percent a year since its modern inception in the 1970s, fueled by the Middle East oil boom of that decade. "There was a lot of hostility when we first started out. We were regarded with suspicion, especially by the regulatory authorities. We were an odd fish. Authorities only acquiesced when they saw the huge demand," said Dar Al-Maal Al-Islami's Al-Faisal, who has been in Islamic finance since the late 1970s.

Islamic finance now accounts for about 1 percent of the global market, according to Majid Dawood, chief executive of Yasaar, a Dubai-based sharia financing consultancy. "We had expected to be at 12 percent of the global market by 2025, but now with this financial crisis, we expect to get there much faster," he said in a telephone interview from New York, where he was speaking at a conference on Islamic banking.

Growth in Islamic banking picked up even before the current financial crisis, mainly because of strong client demand for safe, religiously acceptable investments and a recent explosion in new and innovative financial instruments, said Jane Kinninmont, an analyst at the Economist Intelligence Unit, a research and advisory company.

Islamic banks now offer credit cards in which the full balance must be paid off at month's end. They have devised a kind of commercial paper known as sukuk, which generates a

The Top Ten Islamic Banks, 2007

Rank	Country of Incorporation	Bank	Total Assets 2007
1	Saudi Arabia	Al Rajhi Bank	33,372,165,720
2	Kuwait	Kuwait Finance House	32,103,331,547
3	United Arab Emirates	Dubai Islamic Bank	22,803,738,851
4	Qatar	Qatar Islamic Bank (Al Masraf)	5,877,150,653
5	Malaysia	Bank Islam Malaysia Berhad	5,772,492,125
6	Saudi Arabia	Aljazira Bank	5,762,328,873
7	United Arab Emirates	Emirates Islamic Bank	4,616,888,499
8	Saudi Arabia	Albilad Bank	4,445,428,630
9	Malaysia	Bank Muamalat Malaysia Bhd	4,170,517,368
10	Bahrain	Ithmaar Bank	4,078,789,000

TAKEN FROM: Chris Wright, "Islamic Finance: Size Will Matter in Islamic Banking," *Euromoney*, December 2008. www.euromoney.com.

predetermined return that is called a profit, not interest. It is tied to a specific asset and conveys ownership of it. A sukuk might be issued by a government or a company that is building a hospital or a bridge, for example.

Work in Islamic banking by the King & Spalding law firm has grown roughly 40-fold in the past four years, according to Jawad Ali, a Dubai-based partner at the firm. The firm has 35 lawyers "who do nothing but structure sharia-compliant investment and financing on a daily basis," he said.

Islamic finance first sparked interest in the United States in the late 1990s. The Dow Jones Islamic Index was established in 1999, and the Dow Jones Islamic Fund, which invests in sharia-compliant companies, the following year.

But interest cooled after some Islamic banks were accused of financing terrorism in a lawsuit filed by family members of September 11, 2001, victims, and a lot of Persian Gulf money left the United States for Europe.

In 2004, the German state of Saxony-Anhalt issued a 100 million-euro sovereign Islamic bond. That same year, the first Islamic bank opened in Britain, which now has six Islamic financial institutions, including a retail bank.

> *As banks turn borrowers away in these times of economic turmoil, Islamic institutions continue to close deals in Europe, the Gulf and the United States.*

Although the biggest Islamic banks are in the Persian Gulf—Dubai Islamic Bank, Kuwait Finance House and Saudi Arabia's al-Rajhi Bank—Malaysia and London are growing as major centers of Islamic banking as well.

Islamic institutions are not immune to ills plaguing other banks, such as corruption charges and bad investments. Differences of interpretation between sharia scholars about what is permissible and what isn't also creates confusion. The sukuk market, which had doubled each year since 2004, growing to a total of about $90 billion in bonds issued, fell 50 percent this year after a Bahrain-based group of Islamic scholars decreed that most of the bonds were not compatible with sharia law.

But as banks turn borrowers away in these times of economic turmoil, Islamic institutions continue to close deals in Europe, the Gulf and the United States, bankers said. "Banks feel safer and more comfortable with us because we put down more money, more equity. We are not allowed to borrow with very little down," said Tariq Malhance, a former chief financial officer for the city of Chicago who now heads Unicorn Investment Bank's U.S. office.

And those who have been in Islamic banking for a long time now feel vindicated.

Periodical Bibliography

Shantayanan Devarajan, as told to Stephanie Hanson — "Africa and the Global Financial Crisis," Council on Foreign Relations, October 17, 2008. www.cfr.org.

Andrew Downie — "Financial Crisis: Latin America Hit Hard," *Telegraph*, October 12, 2008.

Ambrose Evans-Pritchard — "Russia Backs Return to Gold Standard to Solve Financial Crisis," *Telegraph*, March 29, 2009.

Martin Fackler — "Financial Crisis Upends the Plans of Many South Koreans to Study Abroad," *New York Times*, January 9, 2009.

Christian Lowe — "Financial Crisis Hits Migrant Workers in Russia," *New York Times*, January 14, 2009.

The Mirror — "Global Economic Crisis Gravely Affects Khmer Migrant Workers," April 10, 2009. http://cambodiamirror.wordpress.com.

Ronak Patel — "Global Financial Crisis Wrecks India's Diamond Industry," *Telegraph*, February 22, 2009.

Mike Pflanz — "Chinese Demand and Financial Crisis Cause Surge in Kenya Elephant Poaching," *Telegraph*, February 25, 2009.

Bilal Randeree — "Is Islamic Finance a Solution?" *Thought Leader*, June 9, 2009. www.thoughtleader.co.za.

Duvvuri Subbarao — "Impact of the Global Financial Crisis on India—Collateral Damage and Response," Bank for International Settlements, February 18, 2009. www.bis.org.

Zarni — "Global Financial Turmoil Affects Burmese Migrant Workers," *Mizzima*, November 2, 2008. www.mizzima.com.

Solutions to the Global Financial Crisis

International Investments Complicate the Financial Crisis and Its Remedy

Michael Mandel

Michael Mandel is the chief economist for Business Week *and the author of the 2004 book* Rational Exuberance. *In the following viewpoint, Mandel points out that foreign investors looking for safe returns on their money invested heavily in guaranteed U.S. funds. When the investments went bad, banks could not pay back these guaranteed returns. If the banks owed money to American investors, the U.S. government could force all parties to come to an agreement. Because the investors are foreign, however, the United States cannot implement a solution alone. Therefore, Mandel argues, an international conference must be held to resolve the crisis.*

As you read, consider the following questions:

1. When did American households flip from being net lenders to net borrowers, in Michael Mandel's view?

2. As the author reports, Lehman Brothers' bankruptcy filings showed that its biggest bank loans came from what kind of banks?

3. According to Mandel, what are the three unsatisfactory options for solving the financial crisis?

I don't know why I called this a "a simple guide to the banking crisis." Really, it's the longest post I've written here. But here it is:

Why is the banking crisis so hard to solve? We stood and watched while Hank Paulson and Ben Bernanke fumbled with their response in the fall. Now we are being treated to the distressing spectacle of Tim Geithner struggling as well to articulate a clear policy for dealing with zombie banks. How come these smart and powerful men can't get a handle on the problem?

I want to lay out 5 simple propositions which will help you understand why the banking crisis is so intractable. Then I will explain what happens next.

Proposition 1: The boom in the U.S. was funded almost totally by foreign money.

This is absolutely the key point for understanding the current banking crisis. Historically, households have been the major source of capital for the U.S. economy. That's certainly what I was taught in economics graduate school.

The boom in the U.S. was funded almost totally by foreign money.

But that quietly changed in 1999, when American households flipped from being net lenders to being net borrowers. Foreign money became basically the only source of capital for the U.S.

Take a look at the chart below [not pictured], which charts net financial investment (adjusted for inflation). Net financial investment for households (the blue line) includes additions to savings and checking accounts, purchases of stocks and mutual funds, and additions to corporate and government pension funds, while subtracting the growth in household mortgages and consumer credit.

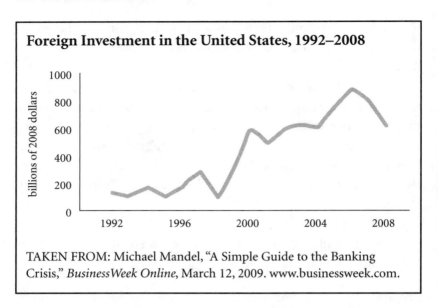

Foreign Investment in the United States, 1992–2008

billions of 2008 dollars

TAKEN FROM: Michael Mandel, "A Simple Guide to the Banking Crisis," *BusinessWeek Online*, March 12, 2009. www.businessweek.com.

Net financial investment for households turned negative in 1999, and stayed that way through 2007 before turning positive in 2008.

To put it another way: In the decade 1988–97, net financial investment for households totalled $2.6 trillion, as households accumulated more financial assets than liabilities. In the decade 1998–2007, net financial investment for households totalled *negative* $3 trillion.

This was an enormously significant shift. This was the first decade on record where households took more money out of the financial system than they put in.

Who took the place of households as net investors? It was foreign money, pouring into the country in the trillions of dollars (see the light purple line). Foreign investors were buying everything from subprime mortgage-backed securities to hedge funds to purchases of shares.

Proposition 2: Foreign investors preferred to put their money into investments that were perceived as having low risk.

Here's the story. Suppose you are investing in a different part of the world. You are likely a bit skittish about putting your money so far from home, so you are likely to choose relatively safe investments.

In the same way, foreign investors in the U.S. flocked to investments which offered decent returns and high (perceived) safety. This demand for safety showed up in the Fed statistics. Between 1998 and 2007, foreign investors poured roughly $10 trillion into acquiring financial assets in this country. Out of that total, only about $3 trillion went into supposedly-risky equities, mutual funds, and direct investment in U.S. businesses. The rest went into perceived less-risky investments, such as Treasuries and mortgage-backed securities (after all, housing never goes down!).

One important reason why hedge funds boomed in this decade—they promised safety to foreign money, which were willing to pay big fees to get it.

But there's more. Wall Street catered to this foreign demand for safety. Many hedge funds, for example, promised "positive absolute returns," meaning that they would do well in down markets. That's one important reason why hedge funds boomed in this decade—they promised safety to foreign money, which were willing to pay big fees to get it. Many hedge funds were pitched directly to foreign investors. When John Paulson testified before Congress in November, he said that 80% of his $36 billion in assets came from foreign investors.

And when there wasn't enough "safe assets" to sell to willing foreigners, the intrepid investment bankers created more. Consider, for example, credit default swaps, which pay off if a bond defaults—in effect, insurance on debt. Wall Street saw this as a 'two-fer.' They would sell corporate bonds to foreign investors, and at the same time collect fees on credit default swaps on the bonds in order to reassure those apparently too-nervous investors from another part of the world.

But the joke in the end was on Wall Street. The foreign investors bought the bonds, but they also bought the protection—which much to everyone's surprise was needed. And the U.S. banks and investment banks were left with piles of 'toxic assets'—the obligation to pay off all sorts of bonds and derivatives.

Proposition 3: Today, after everything has gone bad, many of the counterparties on the other side of the toxic assets are foreign investors, directly or indirectly.

This proposition is based on both arithmetic and circumstantial evidence. The arithmetic is simple. Foreign investors were the main source of funds during the boom years, when these mortgage-backed securities and credit default swaps were being issued in droves. Since not many of these securities are being sold these days, it's likely that foreign investors are still on the other side of these securities.

Moreover, as companies struggle, more details are revealed of their problem. When Lehman went bust, its bankruptcy filing showed that Lehman's biggest bank loans came from foreign banks such as Japan's Mizuho Corporate Bank and Aozora Bank.

Bloomberg reported on March 11 that "most U.S. bank debt is held by insurers and foreign investors."

More recently the *WSJ* had a very good article uncovering the names of some of the banks who were owed money by AIG. These banks received $50 billion in government funds because they were the counterparties to AIG's toxic trades. While Goldman Sachs was first on the list, there were also a large number of foreign financial institutions, including Deutsche Bank (German), Société Générale (French), Rabobank (Netherlands), Dankse (Denmark), and Banco Santander (Spain)

One additional point: Goldman Sachs tops the list of companies that received funds from the government via AIG, but that may be misleading. If Goldman marketed its investment funds to foreign investors, these foreign investors are the ultimate beneficiaries of the payments from the government via AIG. There is absolutely no transparency.

U.S. banks own securities which may or may not obligate them to pay a large amount of money to foreign investors. And foreign banks have assets on their books which no one trusts are worth what they say.

Proposition 4: It's a lot harder for the Federal Reserve and Treasury to resolve a banking crisis where the main counterparties are not American.

The international angle is very important. Geithner and Bernanke keep saying that the problem is that no one knows how much the toxic assets are worth. But that's not the full story. If the counterparties and beneficiaries of the toxic assets held by American banks are also American, it would be relatively easy for Geithner and Bernanke to gather them in a room and make them come to a 'reasonable' agreement about how much these securities were worth. After all, even the most powerful hedge funds must ultimately bow to the power of the Fed and Treasury, especially in a crisis.

But with most of the counterparties in other countries, the job becomes much more difficult. There's no way for Bernanke and Geithner to force European banks, for example, to accept any particular valuation of derivatives or bank bonds—not without the cooperation of the foreign regulators.

In fact, right now we have the worst of both worlds. U.S. banks own securities which may or may not obligate them to pay a large amount of money to foreign investors. And foreign banks have assets on their books which no one trusts are worth what they say. The uncertainty is killing both the borrowers and lenders.

Proposition 5: The fact that the counterparties are overseas means that out of the three options: bailout, bankruptcy, or nationalization—none are satisfactory.

A bailout means that the government makes good on the value of the securities, including the derivatives which are tied to the collapse of the U.S. economy. That means the worse things get, the more money flows out of the country. Not politically acceptable.

Letting insolvent banks go bankrupt is the option being pushed by some politicians, including John McCain. In some ways it would be the cleanest solution, allowing the bankruptcy courts and the FDIC to do the tough job of allocating the losses from the toxic securities.

They tried the bankruptcy option with Lehman, and they nearly broke the global financial system in the process.

The problem, though, is that they tried the bankruptcy option with Lehman, and they nearly broke the global financial system in the process. The Lehman bankruptcy backfired, creating new panic around the world. This reflects how much money many foreign investors had put into the U.S., and how many worried about losing it when Lehman went under.

Nationalization creates a political problem. Once the government buys a company, it is financially and morally responsible for its debts. It puts the U.S. government in the position of either using taxpayer money to bail out foreign investors, or telling foreign investors, no, the richest country in the world is not going to pay its debts.

What's the Solution?

Conclusion: Sometime later this year we will have a massive global conference aimed at simultaneously resolving the banking crises in the major developed countries. The goal will be a political negotiation of the value of the toxic assets, and a clearing of the books.

If the conference succeeds, then it will be possible to fix the financial system relatively easily. But if it fails, then things get dicey.

Protectionist Measures Will Worsen the Crisis

Jaime Daremblum

Jaime Daremblum is director of the Center for Latin American Studies at the Hudson Institute. In this viewpoint, Daremblum suggests that protectionist measures on the part of the United States could result in a trade war in which numerous countries enact their own protectionist measures that are in turn detrimental to U.S. interests. For example, the U.S. stimulus package might foster jobs in the iron and steel industries but trading partner backlash might reduce jobs in the rest of the manufacturing sector. The author believes that retaining NAFTA, ratifying free trade agreements with Colombia and Panama, and pursuing new free trade agreements with Brazil and Uruguay would be good for both the United States and Latin America. On the other hand, if the United States does not pursue these trading partners, competitors such as China and Venezuela will take advantage and build trade interests that are bad for America.

As you read, consider the following questions:

1. According to Daremblum, what is the slogan that summarizes and promotes the protectionist measures for the U.S. stimulus plan?
2. According to Daremblum, what is the significance of the Smoot-Hawley Tariff Act?

Jaime Daremblum, "Latin America Needs Free Trade," *The American: The Journal of the American Enterprise Institute*, February 6, 2009. Copyright © 2009 American Enterprise Institute for Public Policy Research. Reproduced with permission of *The American Enterprise*, a national magazine of Politics, Business, and Culture (*TAEmag.com*).

3. According to Daremblum, what is the Bolivarian Alternative for the Americas?

Is the United States retreating from globalization? If so, that is bad news for countries south of the border.

While there is never a "good time" to start a trade war, the current moment is especially inconvenient. Yet Congress seems intent to push through an economic stimulus package containing nakedly protectionist measures that make a mockery of the U.S. commitment to free trade. The House-approved stimulus plan says that all public works projects funded by the legislation must use U.S.-made iron and steel. The Senate bill has its own "Buy American" plank, which is even broader than the House provision and would cover all manufactured goods used in stimulus-funded public works projects.

On Wednesday, the Senate voted to water down the "Buy American" clause by demanding that it be "applied in a manner consistent with U.S. obligations under international agreements." This was meant to assuage concerns raised by the Europeans and Canadians, not to mention those voiced by President Barack Obama, who on Tuesday told Fox News that "we can't send a protectionist message" and also told ABC News that "we need to make sure that any provisions that are in [the stimulus plan] are not going to trigger a trade war." Unfortunately, even in its revised form, the "Buy American" stipulation may still provoke retaliatory actions from U.S. trading partners. "I would bet everything I have on a trade war breaking out within WTO-consistent rules," Columbia economist Jagdish Bhagwati told a reporter on Thursday.

At a time of economic crisis at home and abroad, a trade war could have disastrous consequences.

The "Buy American" language makes no economic sense. As Gary Clyde Hufbauer and Jeffrey J. Schott of the Peterson

Institute for International Economics have pointed out, it would do very little to promote U.S. job creation. But if other countries responded with protectionist moves of their own, that could have a highly *negative* impact on U.S. jobs. "The negative job impact of foreign retaliation against Buy American provisions could easily outweigh the positive effect of the measures on jobs in the U.S. iron and steel sector and other industries," write Hufbauer and Schott. "The difference is that jobs lost would be spread across the entire manufacturing sector, while jobs gained would be concentrated in iron and steel and a few other industries."

However the "Buy American" debate turns out, one hopes that it does not signal a U.S. retreat from free trade and globalization. At a time of economic crisis at home and abroad, a trade war could have disastrous consequences. That's what happened during the 1930s, when America's Smoot-Hawley Tariff Act—passed by Congress and signed by President Herbert Hoover in 1930—unleashed a flurry of protectionism around the globe and exacerbated the Great Depression.

The Democratic Congress has close ties with organized labor and is heavily protectionist in its attitudes. Indeed, one of President Obama's biggest challenges will be to uphold U.S. support for free trade despite resistance from his own party. Of course, that assumes Obama himself is a free trader. During the campaign, he opposed bilateral free trade agreements (FTAs) with Colombia and Panama and called for renegotiating NAFTA. In his first meeting with Mexican President Felipe Calderón, shortly before Inauguration Day, Obama expressed his desire to "upgrade" NAFTA.

The world is now waiting to see whether, as president, Obama will be more skeptical of trade liberalization than Republican George W. Bush or Democrat Bill Clinton, the latter of whom championed NAFTA in the face of intense opposition from his fellow Democrats in Congress. If Obama wishes to maintain U.S. credibility and bolster America's trade part-

---

Protectionism in the European Union

To revive the economy and curb the rising unemployment rate, leaders of some EU [European Union] member states have begun using protectionist measures at the cost of other member states. . . .

The most obvious example comes from French President Nicolas Sarkozy. He urged companies receiving aid from the government not to move factories "to the Czech Republic or elsewhere" while unveiling plans to help the French auto sector in February [2009].

Liu Xiaoyan,
"Analysis: Protectionism Casts Shadow
over Future of European Single Market,"
China News Online, *April 16, 2009. www.xinhuanet.com.*

---

nerships, he cannot govern as a protectionist. His remarks on the stimulus package have been encouraging. But when push comes to shove, will he risk angering Democratic lawmakers—and powerful Democratic constituencies—in order to defend free trade?

The Europeans and Canadians are eager to know. So are political and business leaders in Latin America. Free trade is especially important to Latin America. In countries throughout the region, U.S.-led trade liberalization has improved economic opportunities, fortified market-oriented democracy, and strengthened the rule of law. At a time of major economic turmoil, U.S. leadership on free trade is critical. Obama must provide it.

He faces at least three big tests on hemispheric trade: whether he will revisit NAFTA; whether he will endorse (and urge Congress to approve) the Colombia and Panama FTAs; and whether he will pursue new FTAs with countries such as

Brazil and Uruguay. The U.S.-Mexico relationship is fundamentally sound, so hopefully any disagreements over NAFTA can be ironed out without upsetting the basic framework of bilateral trade. The Colombia and Panama deals were both signed in late 2006; their approval by Congress is long overdue. Colombia is a key U.S. ally in South America whose government deserves credit for reducing violence and working with the United States to curb drug production.

In countries throughout the region, U.S.-led trade liberalization has improved economic opportunities, fortified market-oriented democracy, and strengthened the rule of law.

Brazil and Uruguay are both members of Mercosur, the South American trade bloc, which would complicate U.S. efforts to negotiate bilateral FTAs but not necessarily stymie them. In 2006, U.S. and Brazilian officials launched a new U.S.-Brazil Commercial Dialogue designed to enhance their bilateral trade relationship. Obama should build on this dialogue and push for a formal FTA. (Admittedly, this would require both the United States and Brazil to make some tough decisions on agriculture policy.) As for Uruguay, in 2007 U.S. and Uruguayan officials signed a Trade and Investment Framework Agreement, which created a U.S.-Uruguay Council on Trade and Investment. Obama should use this as a launching pad to pursue FTA talks with Montevideo.

Whether or not the United States seeks to expand its trade relationships in the Western Hemisphere, China will seek to expand its own. Beijing is moving rapidly to boost its economic links with Latin America. Meanwhile, Venezuelan strongman Hugo Chávez is trying to enlarge his anti-U.S. trade bloc, known as the Bolivarian Alternative for the Americas. If Washington does not make hemispheric trade expansion a priority, it risks losing influence in the region. That would be bad for the United States, and bad for Latin America.

In Africa, Ending Neoliberal Economic Policies Will Solve the Crisis

Demba Moussa Dembele

Demba Moussa Dembele is the director of the Forum for African Alternatives in Dakar, Senegal. In the following viewpoint, he argues that neoliberal policies that push unregulated capitalism have failed. In the face of the crisis, Western nations, the International Monetary Fund, and the World Bank are passing stimulus packages and bailing out banks—the very policies, Dembele says, that African nations were told to avoid for thirty years. Therefore, Dembele argues, Africa should reject unrestricted free trade, nationalize key industries, increase the role of the state in the economy, end debt payments, and look for local financing for development.

As you read, consider the following questions:

1. Whom does Demba Moussa Dembele quote as saying the state was "part of the problem, not the solution"?
2. How much foreign aid was promised to Africa by the European Union and the United States in 2007, according to Dembele?
3. What was the estimated value of the trade between Africa and China in 2008, according to the author?

Demba Moussa Dembele, "The Global Financial Crisis: Lessons and Responses from Africa," *Pambazuka News*, March 19, 2009. Reproduced by permission.

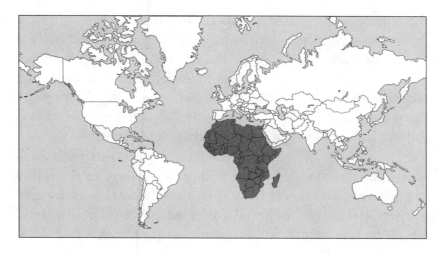

The international financial crisis reflects the collapse of laissez-faire economics and the growing discredit of market fundamentalism. What was being hailed yesterday as the only road to 'growth and prosperity' is now under fierce attack by the same countries and institutions that promoted it for years. In leading developed countries, states have drawn up massive rescue plans to bail out industries or nationalise banks and financial institutions.

Markets Must Be Regulated

The crisis has shattered all the myths associated with the neoliberal paradigm [arguments that stress the benefits of unregulated markets]. It has provided fundamental lessons for Africa and the global South. These lessons should lead to one simple conclusion: a rejection of failed and discredited neoliberal policies and the institutions that promoted them over the last three decades, namely the IMF [International Monetary Fund] and the World Bank.

1) The collapse of market fundamentalism.

The first important lesson is the collapse of market fundamentalism. The crisis shows that the emperor has no clothes anymore. Market fundamentalists claim that markets should

187

be left to their own devices because whatever happens, they have self-correcting mechanisms and that market failures are less costly than state failures. But the reality shows otherwise. The devastations caused by the financial crisis are staggering, as evidenced by the trillions of dollars needed to clean up the mess they spread to the entire globe. And these costs will be ultimately borne by the taxpayer, that is, the state.

Even the most zealous market fundamentalists must have lost their illusions about the ability of markets to discipline themselves and correct their own mistakes. Markets are not impersonal forces, believed to be all powerful and placed above human beings. They are man-made forces whose decisions are ultimately influenced by selfish vested interests.

With the collapse of market fundamentalism, it is the legitimacy of the entire neoliberal system that is being questioned. Even some of its most fervent ideologues are now in disarray. Some of its most sacred myths and dogmas are falling apart. Things that were unthinkable just a few months ago have become a daily reality. Nationalisations of banks and financial institutions, rescue plans for industrial companies, strong state intervention everywhere and attacks against 'unbridled capitalism'; all this is being observed in Europe and even in the United States. . . .

Even the most zealous market fundamentalists must have lost their illusions about the ability of markets to discipline themselves and correct their own mistakes.

---

2) Further discredit of the IMF and World Bank.

The collapse of the neoliberal dogma is a major blow to the international financial institutions. What is even more devastating to them is the reversal of most of the policies they had advocated for decades in Africa and in other 'poor' countries under the now discredited SAPs (structural adjustment programmes). The IMF and the World Bank are supporting fiscal stimulus—expansionary fiscal policies—in the United States, Europe, and Asia. They are supporting rescue plans, including nationalization of private banks and other financial institutions. The priority of the day is no longer inflation but jobs and economic recovery.

Since the 1980s, all these policies were denied African countries in the name of market fundamentalism. Does this mean that what is good and acceptable for Western countries is not for African countries? Whatever the case, one thing is clear: neoliberal policies advocated by the IMF and the World Bank have never been built on 'scientific' arguments but on purely ideological grounds in order to protect and promote the interests of global capitalism. All the neoliberal stuff peddled by these institutions in the South is crumbling with their own benediction. What African countries had been told and forced to implement was standing on shaky ground. . . .

One major lesson for Africa is that they should no longer trust the IMF and World Bank, and for that reason they should not listen to their 'advice' anymore. This is why it is incomprehensible and even a shame to see African countries hold a meeting with the IMF in Tanzania with the aim of building 'a new partnership'. In the statement issued after that meeting, African countries are calling on the IMF to extend its 'experience and expertise' as if African leaders and policy makers had not learned enough lessons from the experience of nearly 30 years of ruinous IMF policies from SAPs to PRSPs (poverty reduction strategy papers).

The State Must Play a Central Role in the Economy

3) The state as central player in the development process.

Another major illustration of the crisis of legitimacy of the neoliberal system is the strong recognition that the state is a central player in solving the crises brought about by unfettered markets, and it will remain a key actor in the development process, whether in developed or developing countries. Some may recall former US president Ronald Reagan's assertion in the 1980s that the state was 'part of the problem, not of the solution'. This signalled the era of massive deregulation and the assault on the state and public service and ownership. It opened the door to some of the most sweeping and devastating structural adjustment policies in Africa. African states came under vicious attacks as 'predatory', 'wasteful', 'rent-seeking', 'corrupt' and 'inept'.

All these qualifications were intended to discredit the state as an agent of economic and social development and the experience of state-led development that took place in the post-independence period up to the late 1970s. Despite the remarkable achievements of that period, the IMF and World Bank used every possible negative example to blame the state for all Africa's crises. They told African leaders that the state was the main, if not the unique, cause of the economic and social crisis in Africa. Accordingly, the solutions they advocated included withering away the state by eliminating or limiting its intervention in the economic sphere. Hence the imposition of fiscal austerity programs, the downsizing of the civil service and the dismantling of the public sector with the privatisation of state-owned companies.

But the financial and food crises show that the state is an indispensable and indisputable agent of development and part of the solution to the current global crises. It is deregulation and market fundamentalism that are part of the problem.

4) Africa cannot count on so-called 'development partners'.

For years, Western countries and IFIs (international financial institutions) failed to heed calls to cancel the illegitimate debt of African countries—debt that has been paid many times over—and that was exacting much suffering on millions of people by virtue of a massive transfer of wealth from 'poor' to wealthy countries. For over 35 years, Western countries have failed to dedicate 0.7 percent of their GDP [gross domestic product] to official development assistance (ODA). Over the last several years, ODA figures have been declining, or stagnating at best, despite repeated claims that commitments would be met. On top of that, it is now a fact that most African countries will not achieve the Millennium Development Goals (MDGs) [of the United Nations], in large part due to lower external funding and declining export revenues as a result of restricted access of African exports to Western countries' markets.

The failure to fulfil commitments toward Africa and other countries is in sharp contrast to Western countries' mobilisation of more than US$4 trillion to bail out or nationalise their banks and financial institutions and rescue their companies in order to save jobs and mitigate the impact of the crisis on their population. And all this money was mobilised in just a few weeks! This massive bailout was 45 times the US$91 billion promised by the European Union and the United States for foreign 'aid' in 2007. The bailout of AIG [an American insurance corporation bailed out in September 2008] alone (US$152 billion) is even higher than this 'aid'. . . .

Africa Must Find Its Own Development Model

Remaining within that paradigm and continuing to listen to the IFIs will only worsen the situation in Africa. Therefore, it is time for African countries to make bold and decisive moves toward an alternative development paradigm. Political will is the key to such moves. Without a leadership willing and able to explore alternative development policies, little will happen. So, the fundamental question is whether African leaders have learned enough of the current debacle of neoliberal capitalism. The other question is whether they are ready to break with it and explore an alternative development paradigm.

1) Discard failed and discredited neoliberal policies.

The first step in that direction is to challenge and reject all the failed policies advocated and imposed by the IFIs and which have cost so much to Africa. . . .

It is time for African countries to make bold and decisive moves toward an alternative development paradigm.

Everywhere, countries and regions are just doing that. In Asia and Latin America, they are taking monetary, fiscal and other measures to mitigate the impact of the financial turmoil on their economies. African countries should also heed this call and take any measures deemed necessary to protect their economies from external shocks.

In this regard, African countries should move to restore capital controls and reverse liberalisation of the capital account [government should not allow the free flow of funds into and out of the country]. These policies opened the door to speculative capital flows, tax evasion and increased capital flight, thus contributing to lowering Africa's domestic savings while increasing its dependence on external financing.

African countries should also discard fiscal and monetary austerity as prescribed by the IMF, because these policies tend to choke off economic growth by limiting public investments in key sectors and by drastically reducing social spending. The stimulus policies, adopted by the United States, Europe and other OECD (Organisation for Economic Co-operation and Development) countries, show that in times of crisis, fiscal restraint has no economic logic. So why should African countries accept fiscal austerity when their countries are in an even worse shape than the developed countries?

Another imperative is the rejection of trade liberalisation and the restoration of protection for domestic markets. In the name of 'free trade' and 'comparative advantage' [the ability of a country to produce a good at a lower relative cost than another] African countries were forced to accept sweeping trade liberalisation that has been very costly in economic and social terms. Trade liberalisation has increased Africa's external dependence, destroyed domestic industries, accelerated deindustrialisation and led to the deterioration of its terms of trade. While African countries were being told about the virtues of 'free trade', OECD countries were provided huge agricultural subsidies erecting disguised or open protectionist policies, all of which have made 'free trade' a joke.

Still in the name of 'comparative advantage', African countries were forced to give priority to cash crops at the expense of food production. The food crisis and Africa's great dependence on food imports illustrate once again that the IFIs have misled African countries into adopting policies that are detrimental to their fundamental interests. The IMF and World Bank, which bear a great responsibility in the food crisis in Africa, are now all too happy to 'assist' African countries in proposing them 'emergency loans' to buy food from Western countries.

African countries should learn from the examples of other southern countries . . . where governments are taking back what was sold off to multinational corporations.

The same IFIs are behind the attacks against the state that translated into the destruction of the public sector to the benefit of foreign capital. They imposed the privatisation of state-owned enterprises in the name of 'private sector development' and 'efficiency'. And private sector development required engaging in a race to the bottom in order to attract foreign direct investment (FDI). To that end, African countries raced to sell off state-owned enterprises, mining industries and natural resources. In several countries, there were even 'ministries of privatisation' whose main mission was to sell off some of the most profitable public assets with little positive return for their countries.

On the contrary, privatisation translated into massive job losses and social exclusion. It may be argued that there is some correlation between the aggravation of poverty and the growing foreign control of resources and assets, because this control is associated with repatriation of huge profits and tax evasion. In a sense, privatisation can be assimilated to a robbery of national patrimony—including strategic sectors— through the transfer to foreign control of assets built throughout years of sacrifices by the people.

Therefore, reversing privatisation is necessary in order to restore people's sovereignty over a nation's resources. It is time for African countries to put back into public and collective hands the control of key sectors and natural resources. No genuine endogenous development is possible without control of a nation's wealth. So Africa should learn from the lessons being given by capitalist countries, including the United States, which are nationalising their banks and financial institutions. But more importantly, African countries should learn from the examples of other southern countries, like those of South America and Asia, where governments are taking back what was sold off to multinational corporations.

Africa Must Reclaim Control of Its Economy

2) Restore the role of the state in the development process.

Reversing privatisation and regaining control of key sectors and natural resources requires a strong and active intervention of the state. Proponents of such intervention have been vindicated by the conspicuous failure of laissez-faire policies and the resurgence of state intervention in developed countries. In Africa, there has been a correlation between state retrenchment, poverty and social exclusion. In a sense, market

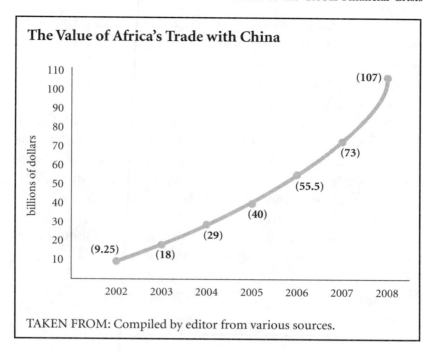

The Value of Africa's Trade with China

TAKEN FROM: Compiled by editor from various sources.

failure is worse than state failure. The national security of a country requires a strong and active state. In fragile nations, state intervention is indispensable to the process of nation-building. African countries should defend public ownership and state-owned enterprises without stifling the private sector. This is one of the key lessons of the failed neoliberal policies and of the current financial crisis.

3) Reclaim the debate on Africa's development.

All the above policies have one single objective: Africa and Africans should reclaim the debate on their development. They should never accept again that others speak in Africa's name. Genuine development is an endogenous process. No external force can bring development to another country. So, Africans should restore their self-confidence, trust African expertise and promote the use of African endogenous knowledge and technology. Since development should be viewed as a multidimensional and complex process of transformation, there can be no genuine development without an active state. However, the state is no longer the only player. It has to contend with civil society, which has become a key player in the debate on Africa's development.

In the search for an alternative paradigm, Africa should revisit key documents, such as the Lagos Plan of Action (LPA), the African Alternative Framework to SAPs (AAF-SAPs), the Arusha Declaration on popular participation, and the Abuja Treaty, among others. An update of these documents and the integration of contributions made by the struggles of civil society organisations in the areas of gender equality, trade, finance, food sovereignty, human and social rights should help Africa come up with its own development paradigm.

Africa and Africans should reclaim the debate on their development.

Is it necessary to stress again that Africa's regional and continental integration is one of the keys to its survival and long-term development? Because only a collective and concerted effort can help Africa overcome the multiple obstacles that lie on the road to an endogenous, people-centred, democratic and sustainable development. So Africa should learn from the experiences of other regions of the global South. The Chiang Mai Initiative in Asia has been strengthened and a new step has been taken to make it a full-fledged monetary fund. In Latin America, the Bolivarian Alternative for the Americas (ALBA) and the South Bank are strengthening the solidarity of the region through closer economic, financial and political ties. These instruments help these countries to resist in a stronger position. Africa has wasted so much time in the process of integration. The crisis should once [and] for all open the eyes of African leaders and citizens that the only way for Africa to survive is to move toward a genuine integration of states and peoples.

Development Funds Must Come from Africa Itself

4) Financing Africa's development.

The external debt crisis, the declining trend of ODA and the low level of FDIs, all this shows that Africa cannot count on external sources to finance its development. Reclaiming its sovereign right to design its own policies goes with vigorous efforts to raise resources internally and shoulder a greater part of the resources needed to finance its development. . . .

So, the priority should be domestic resource mobilisation. African countries should adopt new monetary and fiscal policies aimed at increasing domestic savings. And the potential is huge indeed, if African countries give themselves the means to achieve this objective. In a study, Christian Aid indicates that African countries are losing billions of dollars in tax revenues for lack of enforcement of agreements with foreign companies investing in various sectors, especially in the mining industry. Confronted with weak and ineffective states, these companies resort to various means to avoid paying taxes or pay lower taxes. It is estimated that African countries are losing close to US$160 billion each year, as a result of tax avoidance and tax exemptions.

African countries are losing billions of dollars in tax revenues for lack of enforcement of agreements with foreign companies investing in various sectors, especially in the mining industry.

Therefore, to compel foreign companies to fulfil their obligations and expand the tax base, African countries need to reorganise their states and make them genuine instruments of development. In other words, they need effective states able to enforce agreements and mobilise resources for development. . . .

Remittances [money sent home by migrants from abroad] from the African diaspora have become a growing source of financing. In 2007, they were estimated at US$27.8 billion. They represent 3.9 percent of GDP for North African countries and about 2 percent for the rest of the continent. But for some countries, remittances account for up to nearly a third (30 percent) of GDP. In many countries, remittances are higher than ODA and FDIs. In addition, they constitute a more secure source of financing for development, almost cost-free, while both ODA and FDIs are associated with political, economic and financial costs that are much higher than their potential 'benefits'. So, integrating remittances into a coherent development strategy would reduce external dependence and make expatriates contribute more to Africa's development.

Africa Must Change Its Foreign Relationships

Another channel through which Africa can find non-traditional financing is South-South cooperation. With the rise of new powers sitting on top of huge cash reserves and willing to build a new type of cooperation with African countries, it is an opportunity that should be used wisely. Already, several African countries are turning more and more to these powers, like China, India, Iran, Venezuela and Gulf countries, for loans, direct investments and joint ventures. South-South trade has increased from US$577 billion to US$1,700 billion between 1995 and 2005 and it keeps rising. In 2008, trade between Africa and China was estimated at US$107 billion, with a favourable balance for Africa. By developing its economic and financial ties with the rest of the South, Africa will strengthen the policy space it needs to weaken the influence of 'traditional partners'.

African countries should pursue more forcefully the call for the unconditional cancellation of the continent's illegitimate debt. The multilateral 'debt relief' initiative (MDRI) is not an adequate response to Africa's demand. Only a few countries are included and they have to comply with crippling conditions dictated by the IFIs. If Western countries and institutions do not heed the demand for debt cancellation, African countries should have the right to take unilateral actions to stop debt payments because they violate the basic human and social rights of their citizens.

Along with debt cancellation, African leaders and institutions should join civil society organisations in calling for reparations for centuries of slavery, colonialism, domination, exploitation and plunder of the continent's resources. This is a protracted struggle, but one which can be won if Africa is willing to sustain that struggle for as long as it takes.

African countries should have the right to take unilateral actions to stop debt payments because they violate the basic human and social rights of their citizens.

Likewise, Africa should launch another major struggle for the repatriation of the wealth stolen from the African people and illegally kept abroad with the complicity of Western states and financial institutions. Tax evasions, capital flight and transfer pricing have deprived African countries of billions of dollars that should be returned to serve the continent's development. Therefore, Africa, through its regional and continental institutions, should launch a campaign for the repatriation of that wealth and seek the help of the United Nations institutions, the solidarity of the global South and the support of progressive public opinion in the North.

The financial crisis has accelerated the discrediting of the international financial institutions and deepened the crisis of legitimacy of the neoliberal system. This offers Africa a unique opportunity to free itself from the influence of the neoliberal ideology and the control of these institutions. African countries should have the courage and political will to break with failed and discredited policies. Never before did they have such an opportunity and strong reasons to explore alternative policies. It is time for Africa to reclaim the debate on its development and take responsibility for it. Examples from other regions of the global South provide important lessons that African countries could learn from and use to their benefit.

U.S. Bailouts Are Corporate Welfare and Will Not Solve the Crisis

George Monbiot

George Monbiot is a British journalist, author, and activist. He is the author of Captive State: The Corporate Takeover of Britain. *In the following viewpoint, Monbiot argues that the U.S. government's decision to bail out large banks in the wake of the financial crisis is not surprising. He points out that the United States has always funneled large amounts of cash to big business. Monbiot argues that corporate giveaways result from the fact that corporations spend huge sums of money on lobbying and campaign contributions. Such giveaways, Monbiot argues, are corrupt and should be stopped.*

As you read, consider the following questions:

1. According to the Cato Institute, how much money did the government spend subsidizing business in 2006?

2. According to the U.S. Institute for Policy Studies, how much does the United States spend every year in subsidizing executive pay?

3. According to Common Cause, how much did big banks spend on lobbying in the previous fiscal year?

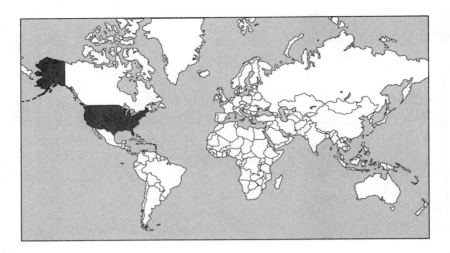

According to Senator Jim Bunning, the proposal to purchase $700bn of dodgy debt by the US government was "financial socialism; it is un-American". The economics professor Nouriel Roubini called George Bush, Henry Paulson and Ben Bernanke "a troika of Bolsheviks who turned the USA into the United Socialist State Republic of America". Bill Perkins, the venture capitalist who took out an ad in the *New York Times* attacking the plan, called it "trickle-down communism".

They are wrong. Any subsidies eventually given to the monster banks of Wall Street will be as American as apple pie and obesity. The sums demanded may be unprecedented, but there is nothing new about the principle: corporate welfare is a consistent feature of advanced capitalism. Only one thing has changed: Congress has been forced to confront its contradictions.

One of the best studies of corporate welfare in the US is published by my old enemies at the Cato Institute. Its report, by Stephen Slivinski, estimates that in 2006 the federal government spent $92bn subsidising business. Much of it went to major corporations such as Boeing, IBM and General Electric.

The biggest money crop—$21bn—is harvested by Big Farmer. Slivinski shows that the richest 10% of subsidised farmers took 66% of the payouts. Every few years, Congress or the administration promises to stop this swindle, then hands even more state money to agribusiness. The farm bill passed by Congress in May guarantees farmers a minimum of 90% of the incomes they've received over the past two years, which happen to be among the most profitable they've ever had. The middlemen do even better, especially the companies spreading starvation by turning maize into ethanol, which are guzzling billions of dollars' worth of tax credits.

Any subsidies eventually given to the monster banks of Wall Street will be as American as apple pie and obesity.

Slivinski shows how the federal government's Advanced Technology Program, which was supposed to support the development of technologies that are "pre-competitive" or "high risk", has instead been captured by big businesses flogging proven products. Since 1991, companies such as IBM, General Electric, Dow Chemical, Caterpillar, Ford, DuPont, General Motors, Chevron and Monsanto have extracted hundreds of millions from this programme. Big business is also underwritten by the Export-Import Bank: in 2006, for example, Boeing alone received $4.5bn in loan guarantees.

The government runs something called the Foreign Military Financing programme, which gives money to other countries to purchase weaponry from US corporations. It doles out grants to airports for building runways and to fishing companies to help them wipe out endangered stocks.

But the Cato Institute's report has exposed only part of the corporate welfare scandal. A new paper by the US Institute for Policy Studies shows that, through a series of cunning tax and accounting loopholes, the US spends $20bn a year subsidising executive pay. By disguising their professional fees as capital gains rather than income for example, the managers of hedge funds and private equity companies pay lower rates of tax than the people who clean their offices. A year ago, the House of Representatives tried to close this loophole, but the bill was blocked in the Senate after a lobbying campaign by some of the richest men in America.

Corporate welfare is arguably the core business of some government departments.

Another report, by a group called Good Jobs First, reveals that Walmart has received at least $1bn of public money. Over 90% of its distribution centres and many of its retail outlets have been subsidised by county and local governments. They give the chain free land, they pay for the roads, water and sewerage required to make that land usable, and they grant it property tax breaks and subsidies (called tax increment financing) originally intended to regenerate depressed communities. Sometimes state governments give the firm straight cash as well: in Virginia, for example, Walmart's distribution centres receive handouts from the Governor's Opportunity Fund.

Corporate welfare is arguably the core business of some government departments. Many of the Pentagon's programmes deliver benefits only to its contractors. Ballistic missile defence, for example, which has no obvious strategic purpose and is unlikely ever to work, has already cost the US between $120bn and $150bn. The US is unique among major donors in insisting that the food it offers in aid is produced on its own soil, rather than in the regions it is meant to be helping. USAID used to boast on its Web site that "the principal beneficiary of America's foreign assistance programs has always been the United States. Close to 80% of the USAID's contracts and grants go directly to American firms." There is not and has never been a free market in the US.

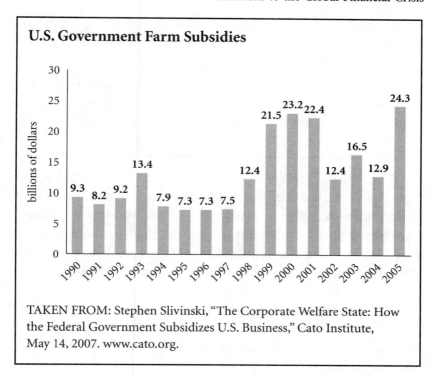

U.S. Government Farm Subsidies

TAKEN FROM: Stephen Slivinski, "The Corporate Welfare State: How the Federal Government Subsidizes U.S. Business," Cato Institute, May 14, 2007. www.cato.org.

Why not? Because the congressmen and women now railing against financial socialism depend for their re-election on the companies they subsidise. The legal bribes paid by these businesses deliver two short-term benefits for them. The first is that they prevent proper regulation, allowing them to make spectacular profits and to generate disasters of the kind Congress is now confronting. The second is that public money that should be used to help the poorest is instead diverted into the pockets of the rich.

A report published last week by the advocacy group Common Cause shows how bankers and brokers stopped legislators banning unsustainable lending. Over the past financial year, the big banks spent $49m on lobbying and $7m in direct campaign contributions. Fannie Mae and Freddie Mac spent $180m in lobbying and campaign finance over the past eight years. Much of this was thrown at members of the House financial services committee and the Senate banking committee.

You give a million dollars to the right man and reap a billion dollars' worth of state protection, tax breaks, and subsidies. When the same thing happens in Africa, we call it corruption.

Whenever congressmen tried to rein in the banks and mortgage lenders they were blocked by the banks' money. Dick Durbin's 2005 amendment seeking to stop predatory mortgage lending, for example, was defeated in the Senate by 58 to 40. The former representative Jim Leach proposed re-regulating Fannie Mac and Freddie Mac. Their lobbyists, he recalls, managed in "less than 48 hours to orchestrate both parties' leadership" to crush his amendments.

The money these firms spend buys the socialisation of financial risk. The $700bn the government was looking for was just one of the public costs of its repeated failure to regulate. Even now the lobbying power of the banks has been making itself felt: on Saturday the Democrats watered down their demand that the money earned by executives of companies rescued by the government be capped. Campaign finance is the best investment a corporation can make. You give a million dollars to the right man and reap a billion dollars' worth of state protection, tax breaks and subsidies. When the same thing happens in Africa we call it corruption.

European governments are no better. The free market economies they proclaim are a con: they intervene repeatedly on behalf of the rich, while leaving everyone else to fend for themselves. Just as in the US, the bosses of farm companies, oil drillers, supermarkets and banks capture the funds extracted by government from the pockets of people much poorer than themselves. Taxpayers everywhere should be asking the same question: why the hell should we be supporting them?

Japan's Experiences Provide Lessons for Dealing with the Crisis

Masaaki Shirakawa

Masaaki Shirakawa is governor of the Bank of Japan. In this viewpoint, he argues that Japan's financial crisis in the 1990s was similar to the current global financial crisis. Japan in the '90s faced bad debts, problematic accounting standards, and an inability to deal with failed financial institutions—the very problems governments face today. To solve these problems, Shirakawa argues the governments must use public funds to buy or guarantee bad assets and shore up faith in the banking system. Even so, Shirakawa says, Japan's experience suggests that recovery may take a long time.

As you read, consider the following questions:

1. According to Masaaki Shirakawa, following the Japanese financial crisis of the 1990s, when did the profitability of Japanese banks hit bottom and begin to improve?

2. According to Shirakawa, what are two options to remove uncertainty stemming from financial institutions' non-performing assets?

3. According to Shirakawa, what might happen if protectionism spreads?

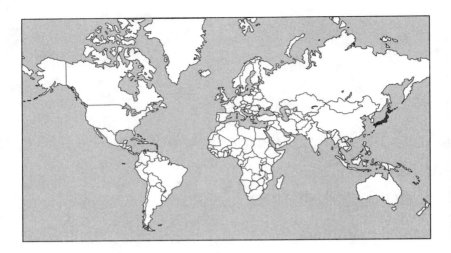

Introduction

I am much honored to be invited to address the 4th Deposit Insurance Corporation of Japan Round Table in Tokyo.

As you are well aware, the global financial system is unstable due to the burst of the global credit bubble. In particular, global financial markets have been under severe strain since the collapse of Lehman Brothers last autumn. Both the central bank and the deposit insurance corporation do not draw much attention under normal circumstances, and their presence stands out only when depositors and financial market participants do not have full confidence in the soundness of financial institutions and financial system stability. Today, the activities of the deposit insurance corporation and the central bank draw much attention from the public, and that is a testament that we are facing difficult challenges.

From a longer-term perspective, it was in the early 1990s when the activities of the Deposit Insurance Corporation of Japan, hereafter DICJ, started to draw attention from the public and the media, and the financial assistance by the DICJ was carried out in 1991 for the first time in its history. At the time, the Deputy Governor of the Bank of Japan was an ex-officio Governor of the DICJ, and I, as a staffer at the Financial System Department of the Bank of Japan, had an opportunity to be deeply involved in the process in which the financial assistance was actually utilized. As events unfolded, Japan had to handle more severe financial crisis since the latter half of the 1990s. Through those experiences, it was shown how critical various functions of the deposit insurance system were in achieving financial system stability. In my address today, I will express my views on how to cope with a financial crisis by comparing Japan's experience and the current global financial crisis.

1. Financial Crisis in Japan after the Burst of the Bubble

During Japan's financial crisis, while real estate prices varied according to the region and the usage, the representative index plunged to almost a quarter of its peak. Banks played a predominant role in financial intermediation, and Japanese banks incurred cumulative losses of some 110 trillion yen, equivalent to 20 percent of Japan's GDP. It was after 2003 that Japanese banks' capital strength and profitability bottomed out and the stability and functioning of the financial system started to improve, when Japan's economy returned to a full-fledged recovery path supported by the global economic growth. In the meantime, the average growth of Japan's economy had been stagnant, compared with the previous decades. While the economy of this period is often called "Japan's lost decade", in my view, such a categorization might not be perfectly capturing the nature of the problem and challenges of policy measures taken to cope with a financial crisis. I will touch on this issue later, but it is true that it took a prolonged period of time for Japan to return to a full-fledged recovery path after the burst of the bubble. Today, I will emphasize three points focusing on policy responses on the financial system front. . . .

First, there was a delay in recognizing the severity of the impact of massive nonperforming assets on the economy. It was a few years after the burst of the bubble when we recognized how seriously the decline in real estate prices affected financial institutions. However, we lagged behind in recognizing how powerful the macroeconomic significance of the impact—or to borrow the recently much talked-about expression, "an adverse feedback loop between the financial system and the real economy"—could be.

The legal framework of resolution, operational procedure, and, above all, public funds to cover a capital shortage are vital in ensuring the smooth resolution of troubled and failed financial institutions.

Second, there were imperfections in accounting and disclosure standards. At present, vigorous discussions are going on about how to cover the expected losses over the credit cycle in terms of accounting. At the time, there was a lag in showing the incurred losses of financial institutions on the accounting and disclosure front. Partly because of that, there was only an insufficient incentive mechanism at play to urge banks to promptly address the nonperforming asset problem.

Third, partly as a result of the aforementioned two points, the authorities could not resolve troubled financial institutions in a timely manner, because of the delayed progress in establishing a framework of resolution to cope with troubled and failed large financial institutions. Arguably, the legal framework of resolution, operational procedure, and, above all, public funds to cover a capital shortage are vital in ensuring the smooth resolution of troubled and failed financial institutions. And it was in early 1998 after we experienced a series of failures of large financial institutions that the full-fledged safety net framework was put in place. It is clear in my memory that, the DICJ in the meantime had been tackling the resolution of failed financial institutions by making full use of what it had in its arsenal. Until the safety net framework was established, there were some cases that the Bank of Japan also played an unconventional role as a central bank in dealing with failed financial institutions by injecting its money as capital.

2. Current Global Financial Crisis

In light of our experiences during the financial crisis in Japan, the development of the current global financial crisis gives me a surprising sense of *déjà vu*. Until recently, Japan's financial crisis has been considered as an isolated event unique to Japan. It appears that people around the globe are gradually coming to understand the implications of the massive credit bubble and its burst through the bitter experience during the current crisis.

First, in terms of "the recognition of the problem", for example, the estimate by the IMF on the total losses on U.S. credit-related debts has been increasing as time went. That typically suggests that the impact of an adverse feedback loop between the financial system and the real economy has also been underestimated in the current crisis.

Second, there have been the issues related to accounting and disclosure standards. While the standards have improved compared with those of Japan in the 1990s, there are some new issues. Those include how to evaluate complicated structured products whose market liquidity is extremely low, and how to incorporate off-balance sheet vehicles. In addition, the traditional issues also persist. The nonperforming asset problem of U.S. and European financial institutions appears to have been gradually shifting to a traditional problem of loans on the banking book. The difficulty of evaluating the loan asset value, when the adverse feedback loop between the financial system and the real economy is at play, seems to be an unflagging issue at any time.

Third, the framework to deal with troubled financial institutions was not well-equipped. It can hardly be said that the process of the disposal of the Northern Rock and Lehman Brothers, was carried out within the sufficiently robust institutional framework. Even if such framework was in place, public capital injection into financial institutions is unpopular among the public in any country. In addition, there is a stigma on the part of financial institution to apply for injection of public capital. Furthermore, it is also a daunting task to identify the amount of losses incurred by financial institutions, which is the precondition for public capital injection. Those were all the difficulties that Japan actually confronted.

3. Measures Addressing the Liquidity Problem

I will now turn to the policy responses when a financial crisis takes place. As I have just mentioned, there are many similarities between Japan's financial crisis and the current global financial crisis. Nevertheless, we are not likely to find a "one-size-fits-all" solution. Therefore, let me point out that what I describe from now will be an attempt to present a conceptual underpinning.

It is . . . a daunting task to identify the amount of losses incurred by financial institutions, which is the precondition for public capital injection.

Both in the cases of Japan after the burst of the bubble and the current global financial crisis, the crisis always surfaced in the form of liquidity shortage. In Japan, the default of a mid-sized securities firm in the interbank money market, despite the small amount of default, triggered a steep liquidity contraction in the money market and led to turmoil in Japan's financial system as a whole. In the current financial crisis, after the severity of the credit-related debt problem surfaced in August 2007, U.S. and European financial institutions faced a liquidity shortage, and the collapse of Lehman Brothers further exacerbated the conditions in the funding markets.

As such, while a lack of liquidity was the starting point of the problem, the root cause of the problem was an issue of the solvency of financial institutions.

In the early phase of a crisis, it is difficult to recognize how serious the liquidity problem is and how serious the solvency problem is. In case it is purely a liquidity problem, which is a relatively idyllic case, the central bank plays a role as "the lender of last resort" based on classical Bagehot's principle. If it is likely that the problem is not a pure liquidity problem but a solvency problem from a system-wide perspective, there would be various challenges in carrying out policy responses in a timely manner. In such a case, while the central bank prevents the financial system from further destabilizing through aggressive liquidity provision, the financial institutions should identify their incurred losses and need to cover the capital shortages in the market, and the government ought to carry out public capital injection when the capital raising turns out to be insufficient.

Put that in the context of the current global financial crisis, concern over counterparty risks intensified to an extraordinary level after the collapse of Lehman Brothers. And not only the confidence of depositors declined but also interbank money markets faced malfunctioning, where a high degree of mutual trust between the participants is a prerequisite. Once confidence collapses, the restoration of confidence becomes a top priority. In that regard, several countries expanded the coverage of deposit insurance and provided a government guarantee for financial institutions' funding in the markets. Those measures were indeed effective. The deposit insurance system is intended to ensure bank depositors' confidence through protecting deposits up to a predetermined amount. In the current crisis, the expansion of the coverage of deposit insurance indeed had effects of stabilizing depositors' behaviors to some extent. Moreover, central banks have been trying to stabilize global financial markets by making extraordinary arrangements to provide liquidity to the markets in the U.S. dollar together with their own currencies.

Through those measures, the funding conditions of U.S. and European financial institutions have been eased to some extent, compared with the situation immediately after the collapse of Lehman Brothers. However, as each government decided to introduce a guarantee scheme and the expansion of deposit insurance coverage, it created some unintended problems. The international flow of funds has changed, and some sound financial institutions that were in no need of receiving government guarantees have faced unfavorable funding conditions. While Japan has not introduced a government guarantee scheme, fund-raising by international financial institutions that received government guarantees, in off-shore markets or in the Samurai bond market in Tokyo, has adversely affected the corporate bond issuance of Japanese firms in the yen-denominated bond markets. In addition, in Japan's interbank money market, it took some time for international financial institutions to raise funds easily, because the coverage and the procedure of a government guarantee were not clearly recognized by market participants. In that regard, during the financial crisis since the late 1990s, Japan adopted a blanket guarantee of all liabilities of financial institutions. While that was an extraordinary measure, it was quite effective in averting the collapse of the financial system.

4. Restoration of Solvency

Together with policy measures on the liquidity front, measures to restore solvency are of vital importance in a financial crisis. In the current global financial crisis, several measures have been already taken since last autumn to restore the solvency of financial institutions by using public capital. Those measures have proved to be effective. Nevertheless, there have been some cases in which financial institutions that received public

Japan's Lost Decade

Japan experienced a disastrous decade of economic stagnation and deflation from 1991 to 2001 after bubbles in its stock market and land market collapsed. While some economic pain was unavoidable—given a 60 percent plunge in equity prices between late 1989 and August 1992, accompanied by the onset of what ultimately became a 70 percent drop in land values by 2001—the "lost decade" was not an inevitable outcome. It required a series of persistently wrong economic policy decisions that ignored the lessons learned in America's Great Depression of the 1930s and the subsequent research on the causes of that painful period. . . .

Japan's biggest policy mistake came in 1997 when the government raised its consumption tax from 3 to 5 percent. The aim was to help compensate for the large run-up in Japanese debt that resulted from the series of unproductive fiscal stimulus packages expended largely on wasteful public works projects. The combination of higher consumption taxes, the continued fall in land prices that persisted in preventing Japan's banks from operating as financial intermediaries because of their heavy exposure to real estate losses, and a rapid return to deflation in 1998 resulted in a virtual collapse of the Japanese economy.

John H. Makin, "Japan's Lost Decade: Lessons for the United States in 2008," American Enterprise Institute for Public Policy Research, February 25, 2008. www.aei.org.

funds continued to face weak stock prices and widening CDS premiums, and thus needed to have the second round of public capital injections.

In those cases, it could be pointed out that pricing of structured products has become difficult, due to the decline in market liquidity, and the quality of loans continues to deteriorate because of the adverse feedback loop between the financial system and the real economy. A "mirage" phenomenon is taking place in that, despite public capital injection, concern over additional losses on the assets mounts over time and such concern in turn will heighten concern for a capital shortage of financial institutions.

Under those circumstances, it is of vital importance to remove uncertainty. There are two options to remove uncertainty stemming from financial institutions' nonperforming assets; the government purchases those assets or provides a loss guarantee to those assets. Nevertheless, even in both cases, uncertainty might not be removed for the assets not covered by the purchases or the guarantees, and investors thus would continue to ask the institutions for high risk premiums. Consequently, the institutions might not be able to fully restore confidence in the market. In addition, there are also other difficulties; how to set the selling price of the nonperforming assets in the case of asset purchase scheme and how to set the fee in the case of guarantee scheme. What Japan faced in the past and what the U.S. is facing now is arguably those difficulties. However, even with such difficulties, it is an indispensable process to promptly identify the amount of losses and to carry out recapitalization to secure financial system stability, if necessary.

Measures to restore solvency are of vital importance in a financial crisis.

It should be noted that new issues have emerged in the global financial system as public capital injection prevails. One of them is a gap between the level of capital recorded on the balance sheet and market participants' perception of franchise value of financial institutions. The level of capital presumably should reflect market expectations about earning growth potential of a firm. On one hand, recapitalization by the government serves as a buffer for future losses, in the same way with privately raised capital. On the other hand, it comes from different incentives from private capital, in which investors shoulder the risk with an expectation to recoup their investments by the future growth of the firm.

In addition, if people increasingly tend to judge the soundness of a financial institution simply by looking at the level of capital on the balance sheet—in other words, looking at the capacity to absorb future losses rather than the earning growth potential—, a financial institution could face a paradoxical situation. A financial institution which does not accept public capital because of its financial soundness might suffer a competitive disadvantage against another institution which accepts public capital, because the sound institution has a lower capital adequacy ratio as a result. Furthermore, if many financial institutions intend to raise regulatory capital adequacy ratios at this juncture in order to avoid such disadvantage, the real economy will be adversely affected. When reviewing financial regulation and supervision in the future, the role of capital regulation will definitely be an important issue on the agenda. Aside from such a general point, it is also necessary to take into account that, during a financial crisis, the regulatory framework of capital adequacy ratio should not amplify procyclicality.

Closing Remarks

I have so far expressed my views on the steps to cope with a financial crisis. In closing, I will offer two thoughts with respect to financial crisis responses.

First, it is necessary to make an objective assessment of what can be solved and what cannot be solved by policy responses to a financial crisis. Both in terms of macroeconomic policy and financial system measures, to take prompt and bold measures to address a financial crisis is not easy for any country, but is quite important. Without those measures, the economies will be forced to experience heavy adjustments and might end up in a perfect storm. At the same time, however, crisis responses do not eliminate the excesses accumulated in the periods preceding the crisis. When those excesses are really massive, it will take long for the economy to return to a sustainable growth path. Japan's "lost decade" was partly attributable to such an element. If protectionism spreads, triggered by intensified frustrations under such dire economic conditions, the economy's potential growth rate itself might decline. In that regard, we also need to make a realistic assessment of the nature of the current crisis and limits of the crisis responses.

Second, in a financial crisis, it is critical to ensure cooperation between the authorities—the deposit insurance corporation, the central bank, and financial supervisory authorities—which are responsible for financial system stability. Cooperation between each country's authorities has also become increasingly important, reflecting the globalization of financial markets and hence the globalization of a financial crisis. Cooperative ties in terms of the nuts and bolts seem to have been furthered during the current crisis. At present, the cooperative relationship between jurisdictions appears to be strengthening at various levels. One element of the cooperative relationship is to share each country's experience and lessons. In closing, I sincerely hope that the 4th Deposit Insurance Corporation of Japan Round Table in Tokyo would offer such a valuable opportunity to share each other's recognition and exchange views between participants.

Thank you very much.

The United States Should Follow Sweden's Example and Nationalize Its Banks

Matthew Richardson and Nouriel Roubini

Matthew Richardson and Nouriel Roubini are professors at New York University's Stern School of Business. They both contributed to the book Restoring Financial Stability: How to Repair a Failed System. *In the following viewpoint, the authors argue that the U.S. banking system is insolvent, with billions of dollars in debt. The only option left, they argue, is to nationalize the banks by quickly determining which institutions are insolvent, seizing them, and selling their assets to pay off depositors. Sweden, which successfully nationalized, cleaned up, and reprivatized many of its banks in 1992, could serve as a blueprint.*

As you read, consider the following questions:

1. According to the authors' latest estimates, total losses on loans and the fall in value of assets will reach about what figure?
2. What do the authors suggest might be a more palatable name for "nationalization"?
3. According to the authors, to whom did the Swedes delegate the details of the bank cleanup?

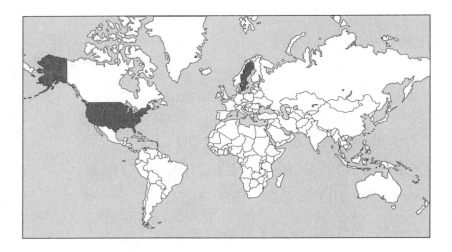

The U.S. banking system is close to being insolvent, and unless we want to become like Japan in the 1990s [which suffered a decade-long recession]—or the United States in the 1930s—the only way to save it is to nationalize it.

Takeover Is the Only Way

As free-market economists teaching at a business school in the heart of the world's financial capital, we feel downright blasphemous proposing an all-out government takeover of the banking system. But the U.S. financial system has reached such a dangerous tipping point that little choice remains. And while Treasury Secretary Timothy Geithner's recent plan to save it has many of the right elements, it's basically too late.

The subprime mortgage mess alone does not force our hand; the $1.2 trillion it involves is just the beginning of the problem. Another $7 trillion—including commercial real estate loans, consumer credit-card debt and high-yield bonds and leveraged loans—is at risk of losing much of its value. Then there are trillions more in high-grade corporate bonds and loans and jumbo prime mortgages, whose worth will also drop precipitously as the recession deepens and more firms and households default on their loans and mortgages.

Last year [2008] we predicted that losses by U.S. financial institutions would hit $1 trillion and possibly go as high as $2 trillion. We were accused of exaggerating. But since then, write-downs by U.S. banks have passed the $1 trillion mark, and now institutions such as the International Monetary Fund and Goldman Sachs [an investment and securities firm] predict losses of more than $2 trillion.

As free-market economists . . . we feel downright blasphemous proposing an all-out government takeover of the banking system. But . . . little choice remains.

But if you think that $2 trillion is high, consider our latest estimates at the financial Web site RGE Monitor: They suggest that total losses on loans made by U.S. banks and the fall in the market value of the assets they are holding will reach about $3.6 trillion. The U.S. banking sector is exposed to half that figure, or $1.8 trillion. Even with the original federal bailout funds from last fall [2008], the capital backing the banks' assets was only $1.4 trillion, leaving the U.S. banking system about $400 billion in the hole.

Two important parts of Geithner's plan are "stress testing" banks by poring over their books to separate viable institutions from bankrupt ones and establishing an investment fund with private and public money to purchase bad assets. These are necessary steps toward a healthy financial sector.

But unfortunately, the plan won't solve our financial woes, because it assumes that the system is solvent. If implemented fairly for current taxpayers (i.e., no more freebies in the form of underpriced equity, preferred shares, loan guarantees or insurance on assets), it will just confirm how bad things really are.

Britain Nationalizes Northern Rock Bank, February 2008

The chancellor [of the exchequer, or finance minister of Britain] Alistair Darling, moved to end six months of turmoil over the fate of Northern Rock yesterday when he admitted his efforts to find a buyer for the stricken bank had failed and he was forced into the first nationalisation of a British company since the 1970s. . . .

Darling . . . defended his handling of the crisis. . . . The government only stepped in to prevent a domino effect in the industry, he said.

Phillip Inman, Larry Elliott, and David Hencke,
"Darling Under Fire as Northern Rock Is Nationalised,"
Guardian Online, *February 18, 2008. www.guardian.co.uk.*

Principles for Nationalization

Nationalization is the only option that would permit us to solve the problem of toxic assets in an orderly fashion and finally allow lending to resume. Of course, the economy would still stink, but the death spiral we are in would end.

Nationalization—call it "receivership" if that sounds more palatable—won't be easy, but here is a set of principles for the government to go by:

First—and this is by far the toughest step—determine which banks are insolvent. Geithner's stress test would be helpful here. The government should start with the big banks that have outside debt, and it should determine which are solvent and which aren't in one fell swoop, to avoid panic. Otherwise, bringing down one big bank will start an immediate run on the equity and long-term debt of the others. It will be a rough ride, but the regulators must stay strong.

Second, immediately nationalize insolvent institutions. The equity [stock] holders will be wiped out, and long-term debt holders will have claims only after the depositors and other short-term creditors are paid off.

Third, once an institution is taken over, separate its assets into good ones and bad ones. The bad assets would be valued at current (albeit depressed) values. Again, as in Geithner's plan, private capital could purchase a fraction of those bad assets. As for the good assets, they would go private again, either through an IPO [initial public offering; a public sale of stock] or a sale to a strategic buyer.

The government should start with the big banks that have outside debt, and it should determine which are solvent and which aren't in one fell swoop, to avoid panic.

The proceeds from both these bad and good assets would first go to depositors and then to debt holders, with some possible sharing with the government to cover administrative costs. If the depositors are paid off in full, then the government actually breaks even.

Fourth, merge all the remaining bad assets into one enterprise. The assets could be held to maturity or eventually sold off with the gains and risks accruing to the taxpayers.

Follow Sweden's Example

The eventual outcome would be a healthy financial system with many new banks capitalized by good assets. Insolvent, too-big-to-fail banks would be broken up into smaller pieces less likely to threaten the whole financial system. Regulatory reforms would also be instituted to reduce the chances of costly future crises.

Nationalizing banks is not without precedent. In 1992, the Swedish government took over its insolvent banks, cleaned them up and reprivatized them. Obviously, the Swedish system was much smaller than the U.S. system. Moreover, some of the current U.S. financial institutions are significantly larger and more complex, making analysis difficult. And today's global capital markets make gaming the system easier than in 1992. But we believe that, if applied correctly, the Swedish solution will work here.

Sweden's restructuring agency was not an out-of-control bureaucracy; it delegated all the details of the cleanup to private bankers and managers hired by the government. The process was remarkably smooth.

In 1992, the Swedish government took over its insolvent banks, cleaned them up and reprivatized them.

Basically, we're all Swedes now. We have used all our bullets, and the boogeyman is still coming. Let's pull out the bazooka and be done with it.

Sweden's Experience Does Not Provide Support for Bank Nationalization

Fredrik Erixon

Fredrik Erixon is the chief economist of Timbro, a Swedish think tank. In this viewpoint, he argues that during the 1990s Sweden did not in fact nationalize its banks. Instead, he argues, Sweden took a case-by-case approach, providing loan guarantees to some banks and bailing out others. Erixon argues, in fact, that the government went out of its way to avoid full-scale nationalization. He suggests that this was part of the reason that Sweden's bank recovery plan was successful.

As you read, consider the following questions:

1. According to Fredrik Erixon, what are two major banks in the United States that many consider to be in need of nationalization?

2. According to Erixon, why can one not say that the government nationalized Nordbanken?

3. During the banking crisis, the Swedish government bought the holdings of what small regional bank, as the author reports?

In the past weeks [February and March 2009] there has been a lot of talk about nationalization of banks or entire banking system. Citigroup and Bank of America are two major

Fredrik Erixon, "Nationalization, Swedish Style," ECIPE (European Centre for International Political Economy), March 3, 2009. Reproduced by permission.

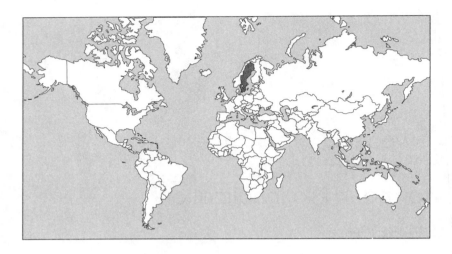

banks in the US considered to be in need of nationalization. The proposition has also received much support—also unexpected support from people like Alan Greenspan [former chairman of the Federal Reserve].

Almost every time such a radical measure to solve credit problems or alleged insolvency in banks (or entire banking systems) is suggested, there is a reference to Sweden's successful experience in the early 1990s with nationalization of banks. The Swedish example is also used as a motivation for nationalization: if Sweden, the mother of soft democratic socialism, nationalized banks without permanently socializing the banking sector, why can't we do it?

I don't think nationalization of the big US financial behemoths will work. But one itchy part of the argument I have particular problems with is the references to the Swedish experience. They are often put in very sweeping terms: Sweden nationalized its banks and reprivatized them when they had been cleaned up. Is this really correct? No. There are many things to be learned from the Swedish crisis policy in the early 1990s. Nationalization of banks is not on the top of the list. In fact, it is not on the list at all: Swedish policy in the early 1990s had very little to do with nationalization.

Sweden Avoided Nationalization

Let me cut a long (and interesting) story short.

The Swedish financial crisis in the early 1990s required actions by the government that went beyond the typical lender-of-last-resort liquidity measures performed by central banks. There was no unified response to banks on the brink of collapse. The government treated banks asking for government support in different ways. One common thread, however, was to avoid nationalization. This was not primarily an ideological call; evidence from other countries hardly suggested governments to own banks.

There are many things to be learned from the Swedish crisis policy in the early 1990s. Nationalization of banks is not on the top of the list. In fact, it is not on the list at all.

The government set up a council to manage the banking crisis. This council inherited some measures that already had been undertaken, such as a government-backed loan guarantee to the foundation which owned Första Sparbanken, one of the high-street banks. They also had a panoply of measures it offered to banks which could not raise capital to stay above the capital adequacy ratio of 8 percent.

The Swedish government bailed out Nordbanken (what is today Nordea), one of the main banks. However, one cannot say the government nationalized Nordbanken—the government already owned it! Nordbanken was built on the various government banks that in the early 1970s were put together into the so-called PK Bank. In the late 1980s, the PK Bank bought Nordbanken, which was then a conglomerate of former small, regional banks. To create a positive commercial atmosphere around this bank, they preferred the name Nordbanken to keeping the name of the buyer, which sounded socialistic and old-style.

Sweden Faces Recession

Sweden is officially in a recession. Not one of those let's ask the public recessions but an economically defined recession of two quarters of negative growth in GDP [gross domestic product]. The second and third quarters in Sweden saw GDP fall by 0.1 percent. . . .

Having been through a similar crisis of their own in the early '90s, people expected Sweden to be able to weather the storm, perhaps a bit better than others. These numbers would suggest that isn't necessarily the case.

Hairy Swede,
"Sweden Is in a Recession," A Swedish American in Sweden,
November 28, 2008. http://welcometosweden.blogspot.com.

At an early point in the crisis, Nordbanken issued new shares which were mostly bought by the government. The government increased its ownership to 77 percent of the bank, but a year later stronger measures were called for. The government bought out all private share holders (partly to avoid being sued for misinformation to share holders when new shares were issued) and split up the bank in two parts (one part became a so-called "bad bank", Securum; another part, with the healthy credit stock, remained as Nordbanken). Incidentally, the Swedish government still is the major share holder in Nordea. It has sold some of its shares, and through mergers with other Nordic banks its ownership has declined. Yet it still owns 20 percent of Nordea.

There were several motivations for this move. Nordbanken was a fairly sizeable bank (one of the Big Five) and a collapse could have thrown the entire payment system into chaos. Another motive was to avoid a malign scenario of falling credibility if the government let its own bank go bust. Furthermore, Nordbanken was the bank used by many government authorities, and in case of a bankruptcy they could have lost a lot of money (at this point Sweden did not have a deposit insurance).

The Swedish government also bought the holdings of the bankrupted Gota Bank. Gota Bank was a fairly small regional bank (it was named after a Swedish region), but together with Nordbanken it was the bank most exposed to the collapse of the 1980s credit-housing boom. The healthy part of Gota Bank was sold cheaply to Nordbanken; the rest was put in Retriva, another "bad bank" created by the government.

Banks Can Survive the Crisis Without Nationalization

But this is as far [as] Sweden's experience of bank nationalization goes. And it is hardly a bed-time story for friends of bank nationalization today in the US or the UK [United Kingdom].

So—what are the lessons from the Swedish banking crisis for crisis responses today?

One key element of the response to the banking crisis was to avoid nationalization.

First, all the big banks had big credit losses, but they survived without being taken over by the government. Nor did they become zombie banks [banks which are bust, but which continue to operate solely because of government guarantees or support], the profitability of these banks returned to high levels only a few years after the crisis started. Hence: if you are looking to Sweden for experiences of how to avoid Japanese-style zombie banks [which became common in Japan during that country's recession in the 1990s] the banks that were not nationalized should be the first stop.

Second, one key element of the response to the banking crisis was to avoid nationalization. The government preferred to use other tools, and they did walk the extra miles needed to avoid nationalization of some of the banks.

Periodical Bibliography

Patrick Bond   "End of Neoliberalism? Sorry, Not Yet," *Counterpunch*, December 26–28, 2008. www.counterpunch.org.

Ricardo J. Caballero   "Constructive Solutions to the Financial Crisis," *Financial Times*, March 16, 2009. www.ft.com.

Carter Dougherty   "E.U. Leaders Turn to I.M.F. amid Financial Crisis," *New York Times*, February 22, 2009.

Michael Hudson   "Bogus 'Solutions' to the Financial Crisis: The Latest in Junk Economics," GlobalResearch, May 22, 2009. www.globalresearch.ca.

Andrew Jakabovics   "Real Solutions to the Financial Crisis," Center for American Progress, September 25, 2008.

Malcolm Moore   "Financial Crisis: China Comes Hesitantly to Rescue," *Telegraph*, October 11, 2008.

Philstar.com   "WTO Head: Trade Openness Solution to Financial Crisis," April 18, 2009. www.philstar.com.

Virginia Postrel   "Macroegonomics," *The Atlantic*, April 2009.

Andy Sutton   "Trade Protectionism Solution to Rebuilding America's Industrial Base," *Market Oracle*, February 6, 2009. www.marketoracle.co.uk.

United Nations   "Solutions to Financial Crisis Must Have Input of Developing Nations—UN Official," May 1, 2009. www.un.org.

World Bank   "African Finance Ministers, Governors Discuss Financial Crisis Solutions," April 24, 2009. http://web.worldbank.org.

For Further Discussion

Chapter 1

1. Robert J. Shiller argues that "boom thinking" is responsible for the financial crisis. Oskari Juurikkala says greed is responsible. Are "boom thinking" and "greed" just two names for the same phenomenon? Explain your reasoning.

2. Which of the viewpoints in this chapter state that the crisis was caused by actions of the U.S. government? Which viewpoints argue that the crisis was caused by the U.S. government's *inaction*?

Chapter 2

1. Andrew Pierce explains that Iceland has suffered badly from the financial crisis; Jonathan Kay explains that Canada has not. Why did these countries experience the financial crisis in such different ways?

2. Based on the viewpoints in this chapter, describe some of the ways that the financial crisis has hurt everyday individuals and financial institutions in wealthier nations.

Chapter 3

1. Based on the viewpoints in this chapter, which countries or institutions in the developing world do you think might benefit from the global financial crisis, and why?

2. In Antonio A. Esguerra II's viewpoint in Devpulse, an official Web site of the Philippine government, he argues that the Philippines has not been hit terribly hard by the crisis. Why might the government in the Philippines want to downplay the economic crisis? In your answer, consider the effect of the crisis on popular opinion in places such as Latin America (the viewpoint by the Woodrow Wilson

International Center for Scholars) and Europe (the viewpoints by Edward Hugh and by Thomas Hüetlin et al.).

Chapter 4

1. Based on the viewpoints by Michael Mandel, Demba
   Moussa Dembele, and Jaime Daremblum, do you think
   that free international trade should be more or less restricted in light of the financial crisis? Explain your reasoning.

2. Matthew Richardson and Nouriel Roubini argue that the
   United States should nationalize its banks. Bank executives and managers generally oppose nationalization, because they do not want to lose control of the banks to the
   government. Based on George Monbiot's viewpoint, why
   might the opposition of banks be very effective in preventing nationalization?

Glossary

AIG (American International Group, Inc.). An American insurance corporation that was bailed out by the U.S. government when it was unable to meet its financial obligations in September 2008.

assets. Anything of value owned by a person or a company. A house, a car, stocks, cash, or equipment can all be assets.

bubble. see "speculative bubble."

commercial paper. A note issued by a financial institution promising to pay a given sum at a specified future date. Commercial paper is backed only by a promise to pay, therefore it can only be issued by well-established and reliable banks or institutions.

credit default swaps (CDS). Essentially, a kind of insurance for investors. For instance, an investor in a mortgage might purchase a CDS from a seller. As long as the mortgage is returning money, the investor would make regular payments to the seller. If the mortgage defaults, however, the seller has to pay the investor a large sum.

credit crunch. see "liquidity crisis."

credit rating. An estimate of the ability of a person, a company, or a country to pay back a loan. Credit ratings are generally assigned by credit rating agencies. The best credit rating is usually AAA.

current account balance. A technical measure of trade balance. Though it includes some other factors, it is based on exports minus imports of goods and services.

derivatives. Financial contracts whose values are derived from the value of something else. For example, you might agree to pay $5,000 now for the right to purchase an $100,000 house in one month. The contract is worth $5,000, and its value derives from the value of the $100,000 house.

Enron. An energy company based in Houston, Texas, which went bankrupt in 2001 amid revelations that it had engaged in massive accounting fraud.

Federal Reserve (Fed). The central bank of the United States. It regulates interest rates, or the cost of borrowing money.

G7. A meeting of the finance ministers of seven industrialized countries: Canada, France, Germany, Italy, Japan, the United Kingdom, and the United States.

G8. The group of eight industrialized nations (Canada, France, Germany, Italy, Japan, Russia, the United Kingdom, and the United States) whose leaders meet at an annual summit meeting.

G20. A meeting of 19 of the nations with the world's largest economies, plus the European Union.

gross domestic product (GDP). A basic measure of a country's economic performance. It includes the market value of all goods and services made within a nation during the course of a year.

hedge funds. An investment fund open to a limited range of investors. Hedge funds have been less regulated than other kinds of investment funds.

Keynesian economics. The economic theory that governments should play a role in the economy, particularly by using stimulus spending to offset recessions. The theory was most famously formulated, and is named after, British economist John Maynard Keynes.

Lehman Brothers. A global financial services firm that declared bankruptcy in September 2008. Its failure is widely thought to have sparked the most serious stage of the global financial crisis.

leverage. The amount of debt relative to its assets that a firm takes on. A firm with much more debt than assets is said to be highly leveraged.

liquidity. The ability of an asset to be converted to cash quickly. A money market account is highly liquid, because you can generally turn it into cash instantly. A house would be less liquid, because you would need to sell it to turn it into cash, or else use it as collateral for a loan.

liquidity crisis. A situation in which businesses and individuals cannot get loans or credit from banks, and thus have difficulty turning assets into cash. For instance, in normal times, assets like your house and future job earnings could be used to get a car loan. During a liquidity crisis, the bank might not lend you money despite those assets. Thus, your assets have become less liquid; they cannot be turned as easily into cash.

mark-to-market. A rule that says that financial institutions have to assign the current fair market price to any financial instrument they hold and trade.

Sarbanes-Oxley Act. A law enacted in 2002 in response to the Enron scandal that tightened accounting standards.

securities. Any tradable instrument representing financial value. Stocks and derivatives are common examples of securities.

securitization. The process of taking an asset that is not liquid and turning it into a security. For example, creating derivatives based on a mortgage or a group of mortgages is an example of securitization.

speculative bubble. An economic condition in which people buy and sell assets at prices far above the worth of the assets. Thus, housing prices in the United States rose dramatically in a speculative bubble, until people realized the houses were overvalued, and the prices quickly collapsed.

subprime mortgage. A mortgage loan to a borrower who is at a high risk for defaulting, or not paying the mortgage back.

Organizations to Contact

The editors have compiled the following list of organizations concerned with the issues debated in this book. The descriptions are derived from materials provided by the organizations. All have publications or information available for interested readers. The list was compiled on the date of publication of the present volume— the information provided here may change. Be aware that many organizations take several weeks or longer to respond to inquiries, so allow as much time as possible.

American Enterprise Institute (AEI)
1150 Seventeenth Street NW, Washington, DC   20036
(202) 862-5800 • fax: (202) 862-7177
e-mail: webmaster@aei.org
Web site: www.aei.org

The American Enterprise Institute (AEI) for Public Policy Research is a privately funded organization dedicated to research and education on issues of government, politics, economics, and social welfare. Its purposes are to defend the principles and improve the institutions of American freedom and democratic capitalism, including limited government and private enterprise. AEI publishes books such as *Privatizing Fannie Mae, Freddie Mac, and the Federal Home Loan Banks: Why and How*, and its Web site includes numerous articles and policy papers on economic issues.

Board of Governors of the Federal Reserve System
Twentieth Street and Constitution Avenue NW
Washington, DC   20551
(202) 452-3000
Web site: www.federalreserve.gov

The Federal Reserve System is the central bank of the United States. It was founded by Congress in 1913 to provide the nation with a safer, more flexible, and more stable monetary and financial system. It produces publications for specialists such as *International Journal of Central Banking* and consumer-oriented publications such as *Consumer's Guide to Mortgage Refinancing*.

Bretton Woods Committee (BWC)

1990 M Street NW, Suite 450, Washington, DC   20036
(202) 331-1616 • fax: (202) 785-9423
e-mail: info@brettonwoods.org
Web site: www.brettonwoods.org

Bretton Woods Committee (BWC) is a bipartisan group dedicated to increasing public understanding of international financial and development issues and the role of the World Bank, International Monetary Fund, and the World Trade Organization. Members include industry and financial leaders, economists, university leaders and former government officials. BWC publishes the quarterly *BWC Newsletter*, numerous policy papers, and reports on its Web site.

Brookings Institution

1775 Massachusetts Avenue NW, Washington, DC   20036
(202) 797-6000 • fax: (202) 797-6004
e-mail: communications@brookings.edu
Web site: www.brookings.edu

The Brookings Institution is a private nonprofit organization devoted to conducting independent research and developing innovative policy solutions. The organization's goal is to provide analysis and recommendations for decision makers on the full range of challenges facing an increasingly interdependent world. The Brookings Institution publishes books on economic matters such as *Budgeting for Hard Power* and numerous policy papers and reports are available through its Web site.

Cato Institute

1000 Massachusetts Avenue NW, Washington, DC   20001
(202) 842-0200 • fax: (202) 842-3490
e-mail: webmaster@cato.org
Web site: www.cato.org

The Cato Institute conducts research on public policy issues to promote consideration of the principles of limited government, individual liberty, free markets, and peace. It publishes reviews and journals such as *Economic Freedom of the World* and *Cato Journal*, as well as policy papers and opinion pieces on economics and other issues.

Center for American Progress

1333 H Street NW, 10th Floor, Washington, DC   20005
(202) 682-1611
e-mail: progress@americanprogress.org
Web site: www.americanprogress.org

The Center for American Progress is a progressive think tank with an interest in values such as diversity, shared and personal responsibility, and participatory government. It publishes materials on economic issues, including business/regulation, credit and debt, the global economy, health care, immigration, and the environment.

Competitive Enterprise Institute (CEI)

1899 L Street NW, 12th Floor, Washington, DC   20036
(202) 331-1010 • fax: (202) 331-0640
e-mail: info@cei.org
Web site: www.cei.org

Competitive Enterprise Institute (CEI) is a nonprofit public policy organization dedicated to advancing the principles of free enterprise and limited government. The organization believes that individuals are best helped not by government intervention, but by making their own choices in a free marketplace. CEI's publications include the monthly newsletter *CEI Planet*, and articles such as "Stimulate the Economy Through Deregulation."

Economic Policy Institute (EPI)

1333 H Street NW, Suite 300 East Tower
Washington, DC 20005
(202) 775-8810
e-mail: researchdept@epi.org
Web site: www.epi.org

The Economic Policy Institute (EPI) is a nonprofit, nonpartisan think tank that seeks to broaden the public debate about strategies to achieve a prosperous and fair economy. The Economic Indicators page on EPI's Web site includes current information about U.S. gross domestic product, family income, international trade and investment, and jobs and wages. Issue Guides are provided on living wage, minimum wage, offshoring, poverty and family budgets, retirement security, social security, unemployment insurance, and welfare.

European Commission—Economic and Financial Affairs (ECOFIN)

Unit R 4, Brussels B-1049
  Belgium
fax: +32-22980998
Web site: http://ec.europa.eu/economy_finance/

European Commission—Economic and Financial Affairs (ECOFIN) is entrusted with the regulation of European Union (EU) economic and monetary policy. Its goal is to ensure the smooth functioning of economic integration in the EU. Its Web site includes access to news articles on the European economic situation and links to its electronic publications such as *European Economy News*, *European Economy Research Letter*, economics forecasts, and research papers.

Heritage Foundation

214 Massachusetts Avenue NE, Washington, DC 20002-4999
(202) 546-4400 • fax: (202) 546-8328
e-mail: info@heritage.org
Web site: www.heritage.org

The Heritage Foundation is a research and educational institute that promotes conservative public policies based on the principles of free enterprise, limited government, individual freedom, traditional American values, and a strong national defense. Its Web site includes policy briefs on U.S. agriculture, the economy, health care, the federal budget, spending, labor, retirement, social security, international trade policy, and economic freedom.

International Monetary Fund (IMF)
700 Nineteenth Street NW, Washington, DC 20431
(202) 623-7000 • fax: (202) 623-4661
e-mail: publicaffairs@imf.org
Web site: www.imf.org

The International Monetary Fund (IMF) is an international organization of 184 countries. It was established to promote international monetary cooperation, exchange stability, and orderly exchange arrangements. IMF seeks to foster economic growth and high levels of employment and provides temporary financial assistance to countries. It publishes the quarterly *Finance & Development* and reports on its activities, including the quarterly *Global Financial Stability Report*, recent issues of which are available on its Web site along with data on IMF finances and individual country reports.

Nippon Keidanren (Japanese Business Federation)
Keidanren Kaikan, 1-9-4, Otemachi, Chiyoda-ku, Tokyo
   100-8188
+81-352041500 • fax: +81-352556255
e-mail: yama@keidanren.or.jp
Web site: www.keidanren.or.jp

Nippon Keidanren is a Japanese organization comprised of companies, industrial associations, and regional economic groups. Its goal is to accelerate the growth of the Japanese and world economies and to encourage innovation. Its Web site includes articles and papers about economic issues, such as "Reconstruction of the Global Economic Chain Needed in the World Economy," and "Mobilizing All Policy Tools to Revive the Economy."

United Nations Development Programme (UNDP)

1 United Nations Plaza, New York, NY   10017
(212) 906-5315 • fax: (212) 906-5364
Web site: www.undp.org

The United Nations Development Programme (UNDP) funds six thousand projects in more than one hundred and fifty developing countries and territories. It works with governments, UN agencies, and nongovernmental organizations to enhance self-reliance and promote sustainable human development. Its priorities include improving living standards, protecting the environment, and applying technology to meet human needs. UNDP's publications include the annual *UNDP Human Development Report*. UNDP publishes *The Millennium Development Goals Report*, regional data and analysis, speeches and statements, and recent issues of its publications on its Web site.

World Bank

1818 H Street NW, Washington, DC   20433
(202) 473-1000 • fax: (202) 477-6391
Web site: www.worldbank.org

The World Bank seeks to reduce poverty and improve the standards of living of poor people around the world. It promotes sustainable growth and investments in developing countries through loans, technical assistance, and policy guidance. World Bank produces publications on global issues, including *Doing Business 2010*, the annual *World Development Report*, and the annual *World Development Indicators*.

World Trade Organization (WTO)

Centre William Rappard, Rue de Lausanne 154
Geneva 21   CH-1211
  Switzerland
(41-22) 7395111 • fax: (41-22) 7314206
e-mail: enquiries@wto.org
Web site: www.wto.org

The World Trade Organization (WTO) is a global international organization that establishes rules dealing with trade between nations. Two WTO agreements have been negotiated and signed by the bulk of the world's trading nations and ratified in their parliaments. The goal of these agreements is to help producers of goods and services, exporters, and importers conduct business. WTO publishes trade statistics, research and analysis, studies, reports, and the journal *World Trade Review*. Recent publications are available on its Web site.

Bibliography of Books

Liaquat Ahamed — *Lords of Finance: The Bankers Who Broke the World*. New York: Penguin Press, 2009.

George A. Akerlof and Robert J. Shiller — *Animal Spirits: How Human Psychology Drives the Economy, and Why It Matters for Global Capitalism*. Princeton, NJ: Princeton University Press, 2009.

Jennifer Amyx — *Japan's Financial Crisis: Institutional Rigidity and Reluctant Change*. Princeton, NJ: Princeton University Press, 2004.

Patrick Bond — *Against Global Apartheid: South Africa Meets the World Bank, IMF and International Finance*. London: Zed Books, 2004.

Richard Bookstaber — *A Demon of Our Own Design: Markets, Hedge Funds, and the Perils of Financial Innovation*. Hoboken, NJ: John Wiley & Sons, 2007.

Roger Boyes — *Meltdown Iceland: How the Global Financial Crisis Bankrupted an Entire Country*. New York: Bloomsbury USA, 2009.

George Cooper — *The Origin of Financial Crises: Central Banks, Credit Bubbles, and the Efficient Market Fallacy*. New York: Random House, 2008.

Niall Ferguson	*The Ascent of Money: A Financial History of the World.* New York: Penguin Group, 2008.
John Bellamy Foster and Fred Magdoff	*The Great Financial Crisis: Causes and Consequences.* New York: Monthly Review Press, 2009.
Dave Kansas	*The Wall Street Journal Guide to the End of Wall Street as We Know It: What You Need to Know About the Greatest Financial Crisis of Our Time—and How to Survive It.* New York: HarperCollins, 2009.
Zachary Karabell	*Superfusion: How China and America Became One Economy and Why the World's Prosperity Depends on It.* New York: Simon & Schuster, 2009.
Charles P. Kindleberger and Robert Aliber	*Manias, Panics, and Crashes: A History of Financial Crisis.* 5th ed. Hoboken, NJ: John Wiley & Sons, Inc., 2005.
Richard C. Koo	*The Holy Grail of Macroeconomics: Lessons from Japan's Great Recession.* Hoboken, NJ: John Wiley & Sons, Inc., 2008.
Paul Krugman	*The Return of Depression Economics and the Crisis of 2008.* New York: W.W. Norton & Company, 2009.
Michael Lewis, ed.	*Panic: The Story of Modern Financial Insanity.* New York: W.W. Norton & Company, 2009.

Minqi Li — *The Rise of China and the Demise of the Capitalist World Economy.* London: Pluto Press, 2008.

Akio Mikuni and R. Taggart Murphy — *Japan's Policy Trap: Dollars, Deflation, and the Crisis of Japanese Finance.* Washington, DC: Brookings Institution Press, 2002.

Paul Muolo and Mathew Padilla — *Chain of Blame: How Wall Street Caused the Mortgage and Credit Crisis.* Hoboken, NJ: John Wiley & Sons, Inc., 2008.

Richard A. Posner — *A Failure of Capitalism: The Crisis of '08 and the Descent into Depression.* Cambridge, MA: Harvard University Press, 2009.

Colin Read — *Global Financial Meltdown: How We Can Avoid the Next Economic Crisis.* New York: St. Martin's Press, 2009.

Andrew Sheng — *From Asian to Global Financial Crisis: An Asian Regulator's View of Unfettered Finance in the 1990s and 2000s.* New York: Cambridge University Press, 2009.

Robert J. Shiller — *Irrational Exuberance.* New York: Broadway Books, 2006.

George Soros — *The New Paradigm for Financial Markets: The Credit Crisis of 2008 and What It Means.* New York: PublicAffairs, 2008.

John R. Talbott *Contagion: The Financial Epidemic That Is Sweeping the Global Economy and How to Protect Yourself from It.* Hoboken, NJ: John Wiley & Sons, Inc., 2009.

John B. Taylor *Getting Off Track: How Government Actions and Interventions Caused, Prolonged, and Worsened the Financial Crisis.* Stanford, CA: Hoover Institution Press, 2009.

Mark Zandi *Financial Shock: A 360° Look at the Subprime Mortgage Implosion, and How to Avoid the Next Financial Crisis.* Upper Saddle River, NJ: FT Press, 2009.

Index